Praise for *Embattled Rebel*

"The best concise book we have on the subject. . . . McPherson is . . . our most distinguished scholar of the Civil War era."
—Steven Hahn, *The New York Times Book Review*

"That Mr. McPherson, the venerated author of the Pulitzer Prize–winning *Battle Cry of Freedom* (1988), mounts a defense of Davis is provocative; the book in which he argues it is quietly persuasive. . . . Mr. McPherson covers a great deal of ground. And there is an economical grace to his prose that makes the book a lightning-quick but lingering read that will appeal not only to Civil War buffs but also to those curious about the Southern presidency and government."
—*The Wall Street Journal*

"[A] fine study of [Jefferson] Davis's military leadership."
—*The Washington Post*

"Superb . . . McPherson succeeds admirably in re-creating the world of 1861–1865 as seen through the eyes of a Southern nationalist and ardent defender of the established social order, and provides readers with a more balanced view of Davis than that handed down by many of his contemporaries."
—*North & South Magazine*

"The first work to discretely consider Davis as head of his armies and navy . . . Crisply written, thoughtfully considered, and ultimately persuasive, *Embattled Rebel* is McPherson and biography at their best."
—William C. Davis, History Book Club

"*Embattled Rebel* is succinct and clearly written. For those who have not read biographies of Davis published in the last thirty years, *Embattled Rebel* is a very fine place to start."
—*Civil War Historian*

"Open minds are in short supply t⊔⊔⊔⊔⊔⊔ ⊔⊔ refreshing that Civil War scholar and Pulitzer-winning ⊔⊔⊔⊔⊔⊔⊔⊔⊔⊔⊔ ⊔⊔ has taken a fresh look at a subject with

"[A] keen analysis of Davis's milit⊔⊔⊔⊔⊔⊔⊔⊔⊔
. . . [McPherson] depicts Davis as a frail dynam⊔⊔⊔

his waking hours buried in paperwork, much of it trivial—a product of his inability to delegate authority—and refereeing the clashing temperaments and tactical disagreements of his generals. . . . *Embattled Rebel* is the perfect title for this engrossing analysis of the True Believer whom McPherson, a Pulitzer Prize historian, calls 'the last Confederate left standing in 1865.'"   —*The Dallas Morning News*

"Mr. McPherson provides a nuanced assessment of Davis as president. The fact that Lincoln's side won, he writes, does not mean that Davis was responsible for the Confederate defeat. 'Most delegates to the Montgomery convention in 1861 believed Davis to be the best man for the [presidency], and no clear evidence exists that they were wrong.'"   —*The Washington Times*

"A well-written book that . . . does a great job giving a simple overview of the major battles while critically analyzing the legacy of Jefferson Davis."   —*Civil War News*

"[James M. McPherson] seeks to understand and explain Davis in his relatively narrow, but crucial, role as the leader of a nation at war. McPherson did the same, brilliantly, a few years back with Abraham Lincoln in *Tried by War*, an analysis of our sixteenth president as commander in chief. His treatment of Davis is equally astute and absorbing."   —Cleveland.com

"A fair-handed treatment from a towering historian and sterling writer."   —*Kirkus Reviews* (starred review)

"A great Civil War and Lincoln historian produces another tour de force as he successfully unravels the Jefferson Davis enigma with precision and insight. The Confederate commander in chief's strengths and weaknesses as a military leader are laid bare for all to see. Often compared unfavorably to President Lincoln, Davis comes through, in victory and defeat, as a leader in his own right. This is must reading for all who have an interest in the Civil War."
—Frank J. Williams, founding chair of the Lincoln Forum
and president of the Ulysses S. Grant Association

PENGUIN BOOKS

EMBATTLED REBEL

James McPherson is the George Henry Davis '86 Professor of History Emeritus at Princeton University. He is the bestselling author of numerous books on the Civil War, including *Battle Cry of Freedom*, which won the Pulitzer Prize, as well as *Tried by War* and *For Cause and Comrades*, both of which won the Lincoln Prize.

EMBATTLED REBEL

JEFFERSON DAVIS AND
THE CONFEDERATE CIVIL WAR

James M. McPherson

PENGUIN BOOKS

PENGUIN BOOKS
An imprint of Penguin Random House LLC
375 Hudson Street
New York, New York 10014
penguin.com

First published in the United States of America by The Penguin Press,
an imprint of Penguin Random House LLC, 2014
Published in Penguin Books 2015

Image credits appear on pages 289–90.

THE LIBRARY OF CONGRESS HAS CATALOGED THE
HARDCOVER EDITION AS FOLLOWS:
McPherson, James M.
Embattled Rebel : Jefferson Davis as commander in chief / James M. McPherson.
pages cm
Includes bibliographical references and index.
ISBN 978-1-59420-497-5 (hc.)
ISBN 978-0-14-312775-8 (pbk.)
1. Davis, Jefferson, 1808–1889—Military leadership.   2. United States—History—
Civil War, 1861–1865—Campaigns.   3. Confederate States of America—Politics and
government.   4. President—Confederate States of America—Biography.   5. United
States—History—Civil War, 1861–1865—Biography.   I. Title.
E467.1.D26M26 2014
973.713092—dc23
2014005403

Printed in the United States of America
1   3   5   7   9   10   8   6   4   2

Designed by Meighan Cavanaugh

To the memory of
C. VANN WOODWARD *and* SHELDON MEYER

CONTENTS

ILLUSTRATIONS

MAPS

MAPS

EMBATTLED
REBEL

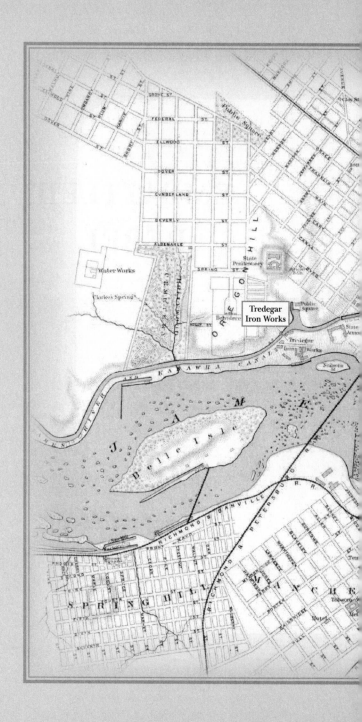

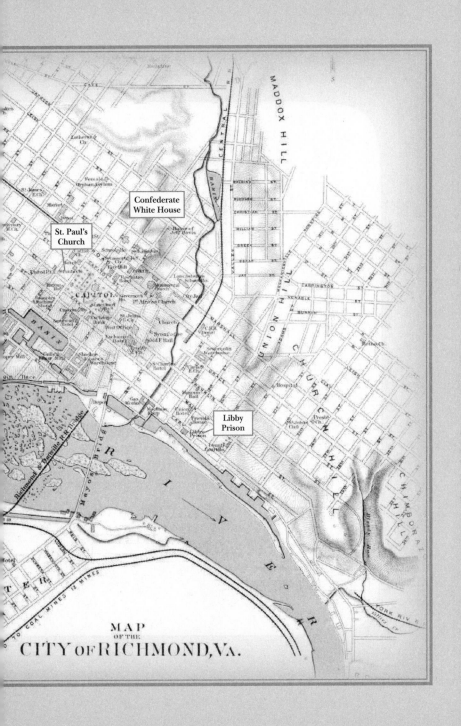

Confederate
White House

St. Paul's
Church

Libby
Prison

MAP
OF THE
CITY OF RICHMOND, VA.

INTRODUCTION

History has not been kind to Jefferson Davis. As president of the Confederate States of America, he led a cause that went down to a disastrous defeat and left the South in poverty for generations. If that cause had succeeded, it would have broken the United States in two and preserved slavery in the South for untold years. Many Americans of his own time and in later generations considered him a traitor. Some of his Confederate compatriots turned against Davis and blamed him for sins of ineptitude that lost the war. Several of Davis's adversaries on the Union side agreed with this assessment. Writing twenty years after the Civil War, General Ulysses S. Grant claimed that "Davis had an exalted opinion of his own military genius. . . . On several occasions during the war he came to the relief of the Union army by means of his *superior military genius*." A number of historians have concurred with this harsh judgment. On the centennial anniversary of the Civil War, David M. Potter famously declared that as commander in chief, Davis compiled "a record of personal failure significant enough to have had a bearing on the course of the war. . . . If the Union and Confederacy had exchanged presidents with one another, the Confederacy might have won its independence."[1]

Comparisons of Abraham Lincoln and Davis as commanders in chief usually favor Lincoln, though rarely to the extent suggested by Potter. The one undeniable truth in such comparisons is that Lincoln's side won the war. But that fact does not necessarily mean that Davis was responsible for losing it. Many factors help explain the ultimate Union victory, including the North's greater population and resources, a stronger economy, a powerful navy, resourceful military leadership, and battlefield victories that blunted Confederate momentum at key points and prolonged the conflict until the weak economic infrastructure that underpinned the Southern war effort collapsed. Lincoln's evolving skills as commander in chief may also help explain Northern victory. I have written about that subject elsewhere.[2] But whether Lincoln was superior to Davis in this respect is impossible to say in the categorical manner stated by David Potter. Comparing Lincoln and Davis as commanders in chief is like trying to compare apples and oranges. They confronted different challenges with different resources and personnel. In the chapters that follow I have tried to avoid the temptation to compare the two leaders. I attempt to describe and analyze Davis's conception and execution of his duty as commander in chief on its own terms and merits, without reference to Lincoln.

Full disclosure is necessary. My sympathies lie with the Union side in the Civil War. The Confederacy fought to break up the United States and to sustain slavery. I consider those goals tragically wrong. Yet I have sought to transcend my convictions and to understand Jefferson Davis as a product of his time and circumstances. After spending many research hours with both Lincoln and Davis, I must also confess that I find Lincoln more congenial, interesting, and admirable. That is another reason to avoid comparisons between the two men in a book about Davis as commander in chief. I wish not to be influenced by personal likes or dislikes. But in fact I found myself becoming less inimical toward Davis than I expected when I began this project. He comes off better than some of his fellow Confederates of large ego and small talents who were among his chief critics. I had perhaps been too much influenced by the negative depictions of Davis's personality that have come down to us from those contemporaries who often had self-serving motives for their hostility.

Many of those contemporaries were officials in the Confederate government and officers in its army. They echoed a Southern journalist who described Davis as "cold, haughty, peevish, narrow-minded, pig-headed, malignant."[3] Robert Toombs of Georgia, who never got over the selection of Davis rather than himself as president of the Confederacy, denigrated his rival as a "false and hypocritical . . . wretch."[4] Another influential Georgia politician, Linton Stephens, brother of the Confederate vice president, sneered at Davis as "a *little, conceited, hypocritical, snivelling, canting, malicious, ambitious, dogged knave and fool.*"[5] General Pierre G. T. Beauregard, whom Davis had removed from command of the Army of Tennessee in June 1862, wrote, "I thank my creator that I am not the essence of egotism, vanity, obstinacy, perversity, and vindictiveness" that he considered Davis to be.[6] In truth, Beauregard was more accurately describing himself. The same might be said of Toombs, Stephens, and others who denounced the Confederate president as hypocritical and malicious. The hostility that developed between Davis and certain generals and political leaders—whether the chief fault was theirs or his—impaired his ability to function effectively as commander in chief.

To be sure, there was some substance underlying the stereotypes of Davis's disagreeable personality. He did not suffer fools gladly, and he let them know it. He did not practice the skillful politician's art of telling others what they wanted to hear. He did not flatter their egos, and he sometimes asserted his own. He did not hesitate to criticize others but was often thin-skinned about their criticisms of him. Davis could be austere, humorless, and tediously argumentative. He sometimes misinterpreted disagreement as personal hostility. Stephen R. Mallory, the Confederate secretary of the navy, had a mostly cordial relationship with Davis. But Mallory noted that "few men could be more chillingly, freezingly cold." In the president's dealings with congressmen, "he rarely satisfied or convinced them simply because in his manner and language there was just an indescribable something which offended their self-esteem and left their judgments room to find fault with him."[7]

But a Georgia congressman who had heard and believed all

the negative comments about Davis changed his mind after a long conversation with him late in the war. "He has been greatly wronged," the congressman wrote to his wife. He "is not the stern, puffed up man he is represented to be. He was as polite, attentive, and communicative to me as I could wish. He listened patiently to all I said and when he differed with me he would give his reasons for it. He was very cordial.... And many gentlemen tell me the same thing as to his manner with them.... His enemies have done him great injustice."[8]

Davis's fragile health may account for these Jekyll and Hyde descriptions of his personality. No chief executive in American history suffered from as many chronic maladies as Jefferson Davis. The malaria that killed his first wife in 1835 struck him as well, and symptoms recurred frequently during the rest of his life. Corneal ulceration of his left eye produced virtual blindness in that eye and may have caused the severe neuralgia that often racked him with excruciating pain, nausea, and headaches. "Dyspepsia," a catchall nineteenth-century term for digestive disorders that in Davis's case may have been ulcers or acid reflux, repeatedly laid him low. He had little appetite, skipped meals, and became increasingly gaunt as the war went on. Bronchial problems, insomnia, and boils added to his misery.[9]

For days and sometimes weeks at a time he was unable to come to his office, but worked from his home and occasionally from his sickbed. His workaholic habits doubtless exacerbated his illnesses. One of his worst bouts of sickness occurred in April and May 1863 during the Chancellorsville and Vicksburg campaigns. He "has not been in his office for more than a

Jefferson Davis

month," wrote a War Department clerk in early May, but "he still attends to business at his dwelling." He had "sent to the War Department fifty-five letters" on various subjects that day with instructions on "what he wished done in the premises. . . . I think he has been ill every day for years, but this has been his most serious attack."[10] His maladies were probably made worse by stress. They may have been partly psychosomatic but were nonetheless severe. Although one cannot point to examples of how his bouts of illness affected any specific decisions or actions as commander in chief, his chronic health problems surely had an impact on his overall performance. And they no doubt helped account for the perceived irritability and peevishness that he occasionally exhibited in personal relationships.

As a wartime commander in chief, Davis determined, performed, or oversaw five categories of activity: policy, national strategy, military strategy, operations, and tactics. Neither Davis nor anyone else defined these functions in a systematic way during the Civil War. If they had, their definitions might have looked something like these: *Policy* refers to war aims—the political goals of the Confederacy. *National strategy* refers to the mobilization of the political, economic, diplomatic, and psychological as well as military resources of the nation to achieve those war aims. *Military strategy* concerns plans for the employment of armed forces to win the war and fulfill the goals of policy. *Operations* concerns the management and movements of armies in particular campaigns to carry out the purposes of military strategy. *Tactics* refers to the formations and handling of an army in a specific battle.

Davis shaped and articulated the principal policy of the Confederacy with clarity and force: the quest for independent nationhood. Although he had not been a fire-eating secessionist, once Davis committed himself to a Confederate nation he never deviated from this goal or compromised its purpose. In a sense, he was the last Confederate left standing in 1865. A vital corollary of this policy was the preservation of slavery as the core institution of the Confederate polity. Davis was a large slaveholder and a consistent defender of the institution of bondage. But even slavery was subordinate to nationhood, and by 1865 Davis was prepared to jettison it if doing so would help achieve Confederate independence.

Although Davis played an active role in military mobilization, he largely delegated the economic and diplomatic functions of national strategy to the appropriate subordinates. Their record of achievement in these efforts was decidedly mixed, with the failures in economic mobilization and foreign policy a result of factors largely beyond presidential control. Davis made several speaking tours to rally public support for the Confederate cause, and he managed to get most war-related legislation through Congress. Growing political factionalism and the alienation of some groups from the Confederate government marked a partial failure of national strategy. Nevertheless, as Gary Gallagher has shown, the Confederate war effort persisted through great difficulties that would have broken a less determined effort, and for that achievement Davis deserves part of the credit.[11]

During his four and one-quarter years as president of the

Confederacy, Jefferson Davis devoted most of his waking hours to military strategy and operations. He was present on several battlefields and even took part in some tactical planning. No other chief executive in American history exercised such hands-on influence in the shaping of military strategy. These activities therefore constitute the principal story line in the pages that follow.

1.

WE MUST PREPARE
FOR A LONG WAR

On February 10, 1861, Jefferson Davis and his wife, Varina, were taking rose cuttings in their garden at Brierfield, the Davis plantation on the rich bottomland along a looping bend in the Mississippi River. Three weeks earlier, just recovered from an illness that had kept him in bed for several days, Davis had resigned his seat in the United States Senate when he received official word of Mississippi's secession from the Union. He and his family had made their way home slowly, stopping on January 28 at the state capital in Jackson, where Davis learned that he had been named major general of the Army of Mississippi. It was a position congenial to his desires. As a graduate of West Point, an officer in the regular army for seven years, commander of a volunteer regiment in the Mexican-American War, secretary of war in the Franklin Pierce administration, and chairman of the Senate Committee on Military Affairs, Davis had vast and varied military experience qualifying him for such a position. He immediately set to work to reorganize and expand the state militia to meet a potential invasion threat from the United States Army. Davis also anticipated the possibility that the convention of delegates from six seceded states meeting in Montgomery, Alabama, might choose him as general-in-chief of the soon-to-be-created army of the Confederate States of America. But for now he was careworn and exhausted. He wanted only to get home to restore his health and energy, supervise his 113 slaves as they prepared Brierfield for the year's cotton planting, and relax by working in his flower and vegetable gardens.

While Jefferson and Varina were taking rose cuttings that pleasant February day, a special messenger arrived from Vicksburg. He handed Davis a telegram. Varina watched her husband as he opened and read it. His face blanched, she recalled. "After a few minutes painful silence" he told her, "as a man might speak of a sentence of death," that the convention at Montgomery had unanimously elected him provisional president of the Confederacy—not general-in-chief but commander in chief with all of its political as well as military responsibilities and vexations. He did not want the job. He had expected it to go to Howell Cobb of Georgia. But the convention, anticipating the possibility of war with the United States, had chosen Davis in considerable part *because* of his military qualifications, which none of the other leading candidates (including Cobb) possessed. Despite his misgivings, Davis's strong sense of duty compelled him to accept the call. He prepared to leave for Montgomery the next day.[1]

Varina Davis

On his way to the Confederate capital, Davis gave twenty-five whistle-stop speeches. While he publicly expressed hopes that his new government would remain at peace with the United States, he told Governor Francis Pickens of South Carolina that he believed "a peaceful solution of our difficulties was not to be anticipated, and therefore my thoughts have been directed to the manner of rendering force effective."[2] One such means was to threaten the North with invasion if it dared to make war on the Confederacy. "There will be no war in our territory," he told a cheering crowd in Jackson, Mississippi, on February 12. "It will be carried into the enemy's territory." At Stevenson, Alabama, two days later, Davis vowed to extend war "where food for the sword and torch await the armies. . . . Grass will grow in the northern cities where pavements have been worn off by the tread of commerce."[3] When he arrived at the railroad station in Montgomery on February 16, he pledged to the waiting crowd that if the North tried to coerce the Confederate states back into the Union, the Confederates would make the Northerners "smell Southern powder and feel Southern steel." More soberly, in his brief inaugural address on February 18, Davis referred five times to the possibility of war and the need to create an army and a navy to meet the challenge. If "passion or lust for dominion" should cause the United States to wage war on the Confederacy, "we must prepare to meet the emergency and maintain, by the final arbitrament of the sword, the position which we have assumed among the nations of the earth."[4]

Davis and the convention delegates, who reconstituted themselves as a provisional Congress, suited action to words. On

February 26 the new president signed a law creating the infra-structure of a Confederate army: Ordnance, Quartermaster, Medical, and other staff departments modeled on those of the regular United States Army, with which Davis was familiar from his years as secretary of war. Subsequent legislation provided for the enlistment of volunteers to serve one year in the provisional army. They were to be organized into regiments by states, with company and sometimes regimental officers elected by the men and appointed by governors. Brigadier generals would be appointed by the president. Under this legislation a small army and even a navy began to take shape.

In this process Davis played a hands-on role, with every aspect of military organization passing across his desk and receiving his approval or disapproval. At this stage of his tenure as commander in chief, such micromanagement was a virtue because the Confederacy was inventing itself from scratch and Davis knew more about organizing and administering an army than any other Southerner. It was also a necessity because his initial choice as secretary of war, Leroy P. Walker of Alabama, was a poor administrator and was soon overwhelmed by the task. Davis had selected him mainly for reasons of political geography: Each of his six cabinet members came from one of the original seven Confederate states (including Texas when it soon joined the Confederacy), with Davis himself from the seventh. The president assigned Florida's cabinet post to Stephen R. Mallory as secretary of the navy. Mallory turned out to be an excellent choice, for he created a navy out of virtually nothing. Under his leadership it pioneered in such technological innovations as ironclads, torpedoes (mines), and even a primitive submarine.

Armed forces need not only men; they also need arms and ammunition, shoes and clothing, all the accoutrements of soldiers and the capacity to transport them where needed to sustain hundreds of thousands of men who are removed from the production and transport of this matériel by their presence in the armed forces. Slavery gave the Confederacy one advantage in this respect: The slaves constituted a large percentage of the labor force in the Confederate states, and by staying on the job they freed white men for the army. But the slaves worked mainly in agriculture growing cotton and other staple crops primarily for export. In the production of the potential matériel of war, the seven Confederate states began life at a huge disadvantage. Even with the secession of four more slave states after the firing on Fort Sumter (to be discussed below), the Confederacy would possess only 12 percent as much industrial capacity as the Union states. In certain industries vital to military production, Northern superiority was even more decisive. According to the 1860 census, Union states had eleven times as many ships and boats as the Confederacy and produced fifteen times as much iron, seventeen times as many textile goods, twenty-four times as many locomotives, and thirty-two times as many firearms. The Union had more than twice the density of railroad mileage per square mile and several times the amount of rolling stock.

From his experience as secretary of war and chairman of the Senate Committee on Military Affairs in the 1850s, Davis was acutely aware of these statistics. He also knew that the state arsenals seized by Southern militias contained mostly old and out-of-repair weapons. Despite his boast that Confederates would make Northerners smell Southern powder and feel Southern steel if they tried to subjugate the Confederacy, Davis knew that he had little powder and less steel. Three days after his inauguration as Confederate president, he sent Raphael Semmes of Alabama to the North to buy weapons and arms-making machinery.[5] A veteran of almost thirty years in the United States Navy who would soon become the Confederacy's most dashing sea captain, Semmes also proved adept at this initial assignment that Davis gave him. But the onset of war two months later soon overwhelmed the limited matériel that Semmes was able to acquire. For the first year of the war—and often thereafter—Davis's strategic options as commander in chief would be severely constrained by persistent deficiencies in arms, accoutrements, transportation, and industrial capacity. Fast steamships carrying war matériel and trying to evade the ever-tightening Union blockade, and a crash program to build up war industries in the South, would only partly remedy these deficiencies.

WHILE SEMMES WAS IN THE NORTH BUYING ARMS, DAVIS was confronting his first crucial decision as commander in chief: what to do about the two principal forts in Confederate harbors still held by soldiers of the United States Army. When South Carolina seceded on December 20, 1860, the commander of the army garrison at Fort Moultrie, Maj. Robert Anderson, grew apprehensive that the hotheaded Charleston militia would attack this obsolete fort. On the night of December 26, Anderson secretly moved the garrison to the uncompleted but immensely strong Fort Sumter on an artificial island at the entrance to the harbor. The outraged Carolinians denounced this movement as a violation of their sovereignty, and sent commissioners to President James Buchanan in Washington to demand that the fort be turned over to the state. The previously pliable Buchanan surprised them by saying no. His administration even sent an unarmed merchant steamer, the *Star of the West*, with reinforcements for Fort Sumter, but it was turned back by South Carolina artillery.

Meanwhile, when Florida seceded in January her militia seized two outdated forts on the mainland at Pensacola. But the stronger Fort Pickens on Santa Rosa Island controlling the entrance to the harbor remained in Union hands. Tense standoffs at both Fort Sumter and Fort Pickens had persisted for several weeks when the Confederate government organized itself and Davis became president in February. The Congress in Montgomery instructed him to obtain control of these forts by negotiations if possible or by force if necessary. Davis sent commissioners to Washington to negotiate. He also named Pierre G. T. Beauregard and Braxton Bragg as the Confederacy's first two brigadier generals and sent them to Charleston and Pensacola to take over the state militias, absorb them into the new Confederate army, and prepare to attack the forts if required.[6]

The incoming Lincoln administration refused to meet officially with the Confederate commissioners. But Secretary

*Montgomery, Alabama: The first capital
of the Confederacy*

of State William H. Seward, who expected to be the "premier" of the administration, informed them through an intermediary that he was working to get the troops removed from Fort Sumter in the interest of preserving peace. Seward hoped that such a gesture of conciliation might be a first step in a gradual process of wooing the seceded states back into the Union. General-in-Chief Winfield Scott of the United States Army supported Seward's position, as did a majority of Lincoln's cabinet at first.

Jefferson Davis would have been quite happy if Seward had succeeded in his efforts to get the garrison out of Sumter. But he repudiated any notion that this gesture might lead to reunion; on the contrary, he would have seen it as a recognition of Confederate sovereignty. That is how Abraham Lincoln saw it too. Fort Sumter had become the symbol of competing claims of sovereignty. So long as the American flag flew over the fort, the Confederate claim to be an independent nation was invalid. The same was true of Fort Pickens, and Davis instructed General Bragg to prepare to attack it if and when an actual attack order came.[7]

But no such order ever went to Bragg. The standoff at Sumter eclipsed the situation at Pensacola in the eyes of both Northerners and Southerners. When Lincoln informed South Carolina governor Francis Pickens of his intent to resupply the garrison at Fort Sumter, he forced Davis's hand. If the Confederates allowed the supplies to go in, they would lose face in this symbolic battle of sovereignties. If they fired on the relief boats or on the fort, they would stand convicted of starting a war, thereby uniting a divided North. But Davis had reason to believe that an actual shooting war would bring more slave states into the Confederacy to stand with their Southern brethren against Yankee "coercion." In any case, he was convinced that he could not yield his demand for the surrender of Fort Sumter without in effect yielding the Confederate claim to nationhood. At a tense meeting of the Confederate cabinet on April 8, a majority (evidently excepting only Secretary of State Robert Toombs) agreed with Davis. From Montgomery went a telegram to General Beauregard: Demand the evacuation of Sumter, and if it was refused, open fire. Beauregard sent his ultimatum; it was rejected; Confederate guns began shooting at 4:30 A.M. on April 12; the American flag was lowered in surrender two days later; and the war came.[8]

Lincoln's call for troops to suppress a rebellion prompted four more slave states, led by Virginia, to join the Confederacy. Neither Lincoln nor Davis could foresee the huge and destructive scale of the war that ensued. But neither shared the opinions widespread among their respective publics that it would be a short war and an easy victory for their own side. "The people here are all in fine spirits," wrote the wife of a Texas member of the provisional Congress two weeks after the firing on Fort Sumter. "No one doubts our success."[9] Davis tried to discourage such optimism. "We must prepare for a long war" and perhaps "unmerciful reverses at first," he said to one overconfident friend. Davis scotched the notion that one Southerner could lick three Yankees. "Only fools doubted the courage of the Yankees to fight," he declared, "and now we have stung their pride—we have roused them till they will fight like devils."[10]

The original bill in Congress to create a Confederate army had authorized enlistments for six months. Davis had objected, insisting that it took at least that long to train a soldier, and urged a three-year term. Congress balked, and they finally compromised on one year. After Fort Sumter, Davis pressed Congress to enlarge the army and to require three-year terms for new recruits. As administered, this law allowed enlistees who supplied their own arms and equipment to sign up for one year; those who were equipped by the government would serve three years.[11]

As this recruitment policy suggests, a shortage of weapons and accoutrements plagued the rapidly growing Confederate army in 1861. The capture of the Norfolk navy yard on April 20 provided a windfall of 1,200 cannon, many of which were soon on their way to the dozens of forts already existing or under construction across the South. The army also could obtain plenty of horses and mules for transportation. Effective small arms and field artillery, however, were in woefully short supply. By July 1 the Confederacy had at least one hundred thousand men in its armies, many of them armed with shotguns and squirrel rifles. The War Department could have accepted thousands more had it been able to equip them.

What were these soldiers expected to do? In his message on April 29 to a special session of the provisional Congress, Davis said no more about carrying the war into the North. Instead, he

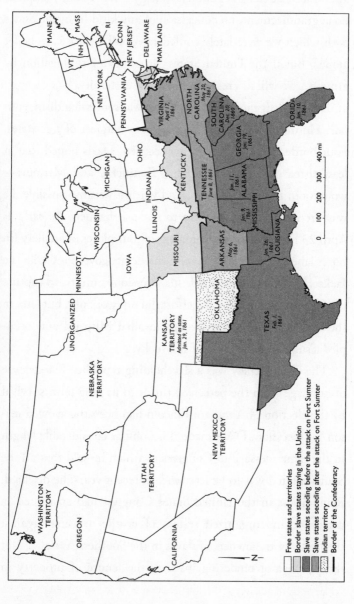

THE FORMATION OF THE CONFEDERACY

MAINE
VT
NH
MASS
RI
CONN
NEW YORK
NEW JERSEY
PENNSYLVANIA
DELAWARE
MARYLAND
VIRGINIA
April 17,
1861
NORTH
CAROLINA
May 20,
1861
SOUTH
CAROLINA
Dec. 20,
1860
GEORGIA
Jan. 19,
1861
FLORIDA
Jan. 10,
1861
OHIO
MICHIGAN
INDIANA
ILLINOIS
WISCONSIN
KENTUCKY
TENNESSEE
June 8, 1861
ALABAMA
Jan. 11,
1861
MISSISSIPPI
Jan. 9,
1861
MINNESOTA
IOWA
MISSOURI
ARKANSAS
May 6,
1861
LOUISIANA
Jan. 26,
1861
OKLAHOMA
KANSAS
TERRITORY
Admitted as state,
Jan. 29, 1861
TEXAS
Feb. 1,
1861
UNORGANIZED
NEBRASKA
TERRITORY
NEW MEXICO
TERRITORY
WASHINGTON
TERRITORY
OREGON
UTAH
TERRITORY
CALIFORNIA

0   100   200   300   400 mi

—N—

Free states and territories
Border slave states staying in the Union
Slave states seceding before the attack on Fort Sumter
Slave states seceding after the attack on Fort Sumter
Indian territory
Border of the Confederacy

announced a defensive national strategy: "We seek no conquest, no aggrandizement, no concession of any kind from the States with which we were lately confederated; all we ask is to be let alone." But if the United States "attempt our subjugation by arms . . . we will . . . resist to the direst extremity."[12]

Davis's pledge to seek no conquest was somewhat disingenuous. He meant no aggrandizement or conquest of *free* states. Four border slave states had not seceded. Davis hoped that at least three of them—Maryland, Kentucky, and Missouri—would join the Confederacy. And when it became possible, he was prepared to invade them to make it happen. As early as April 23 he approved the shipment of four pieces of artillery (in boxes labeled "marble") to pro-Confederate governor Claiborne Jackson of Missouri to enable his secessionist militia to capture the St. Louis arsenal.[13] That effort did not work out, but later in the summer Confederate troops invaded Missouri and occupied a substantial portion of Kentucky.

The Confederacy was a slaveholding republic. The defense of bondage from the perceived threat to its long-term survival by the election of Abraham Lincoln had been the avowed reason for secession. Davis made this point at considerable length in the same message to Congress in which he said that all the South wanted was to be let alone. In recent years, he declared, Republicans in the United States Congress had advocated "a persistent and organized system of hostile measures against the rights of the owners of slaves in the Southern States . . . for the purpose of rendering insecure the tenure of property in slaves . . . and reducing those States which held slaves to a condition of inferiority." In 1860 a party came to power vowing "to legislate to the prejudice, detriment, or discouragement of the owners of that species of property" and to use "its power for the total exclusion of the slave States from all participation in the benefits of the public domain." This policy would result in "annihilating in effect property worth thousands of millions of dollars" and "rendering the property in slaves so insecure as to be comparatively worthless."[14]

One man whose property, Davis feared, might become comparatively worthless was Jefferson Davis. His 113 slaves were probably worth about $80,000 in 1860—the equivalent of several million dollars today. Another was his brother Joseph, twenty-four years older than Jefferson and something of a father figure who had helped Jefferson get his start as a planter twenty-five years earlier. Although the Davises were benign masters who treated their chattels with a degree of liberality, they were also proslavery partisans of the John C. Calhoun school. As a United States senator, Jefferson Davis had opposed the admission of California as a free state because he thought slavery could take root there. He wanted to annex Cuba in order to add a large new slave state to the Union. In an 1848 speech challenging antislavery senators, he declared that "if this is to be made the centre from which civil war is to radiate, here let the conflict begin." During the election campaign of 1860, Davis told the people of Vicksburg that if an abolitionist president (Lincoln) was elected, he "would rather appeal to the God of Battles at once" and "welcome the invader to the harvest of death . . . than attempt to live longer in such a Union."[15]

Davis's conviction that slavery gave "the planting states" a "common interest of such magnitude" sustained his determination to eventually bring the border states into the Confederacy.[16] But his first task was to devise a military strategy to defend the eleven states that constituted that entity in May 1861 from the buildup of Northern power to "subjugate" the South. Such a strategy would be grounded in an important reality, so obvious that its importance is often overlooked: The Confederacy began the war in firm military and political control of nearly all the territory in those eleven states. Such control is rarely the case in civil wars or revolutions, which typically require rebels or revolutionaries to fight to gain dominion over land or government or both. With a functioning government and an army already mobilized or mobilizing in May 1861, the Confederacy embraced more than 750,000 square miles in which not a single enemy soldier was to be found except at Fort Pickens and in Virginia at Fort Monroe and Alexandria across the Potomac River from Washington. All the Confederates had to do to "win" the war was to hold on to what they already had.

To accomplish that, Davis's army was spread around the perimeter of those 750,000 square miles in numerous detachments guarding key strategic points—and some that were less strategic militarily but important politically. Historians have applied various labels to this strategy: perimeter defense; dispersed defense; cordon defense; extended defense. Many of these historians are critical of the strategy because it seemed to violate the principle of concentration of force. Dispersal created the possibility that the enemy, superior in numbers, might break through this thin gray line somewhere, cutting off and perhaps capturing one or more of these small armies and penetrating as far into Confederate territory as if it had been left undefended. Davis recognized this danger. He hoped partly to offset it by using the Confederacy's advantage of interior lines to concentrate forces at the point of a major attack before the enemy could break through. Sometimes that worked, as in the case of the Battle of Manassas in July 1861; sometimes it did not, as in the cases of Union penetration at several locations in early 1862.

In any event, several considerations governed the adoption of the dispersed defense in 1861. The need to protect slavery seemed to require the defense of every foot of slave territory from the presence of Union soldiers, who would attract slaves from the surrounding countryside like a magnet. This attraction began at Fort Monroe in the first weeks of the war, and continued to escalate wherever Union armies set foot on Southern soil and Union navy ships moved up Southern rivers. Confederate diplomats hoped to achieve foreign recognition of their new nation, but to yield any part of it to enemy occupation in order to concentrate forces elsewhere might undermine that hope. The loss of territory also meant the loss of its resources and perhaps the desertion of soldiers from those areas. As Davis noted later in the war, "the general truth that power is

THE CONFEDERACY'S PERIMETER DEFENSE IN 1861

■ Troop units ranging from a few hundred to several thousand men

DE
MD
Washington
Winchester
Fredericksburg
Richmond
VIRGINIA
LATER WEST VIRGINIA
OHIO
INDIANA
KENTUCKY
Bowling Green
Fort Donelson
Fort Henry
Fort Pillow
Nashville
TENNESSEE
Columbus
Memphis
MISSOURI
ARKANSAS
MISSISSIPPI
Vicksburg
ALABAMA
GEORGIA
NORTH CAROLINA
SOUTH CAROLINA
Wilmington–Fort Fisher
Fort Sumter
Fort Royal
Fort Pulaski
Jacksonville
FLORIDA
Pensacola
Mobile
New Orleans
LOUISIANA
TEXAS
Galveston

N

0   50   100   150 mi

increased by the concentration of an army is under our peculiar circumstances subject to modification. The evacuation of any portion of territory involves not only the loss of supplies but in every instance has been attended by a greater or less loss of troops."[17]

The main reason for dispersal in 1861, however, was political—and politics was an essential part of national strategy. Southern states had seceded individually on the principle that the sovereignty of each state was superior to that of any other entity. The very name of the new nation, the *Confederate* States of America, implied an association of still-sovereign entities. This principle was recognized in the Confederate Constitution, which was ratified by "each State acting in its sovereign and independent character." The governor of each state also insisted that its borders must be defended against invasion. If Davis had pursued a strategy of concentrating Confederate armies at two or three key points, leaving other areas open to enemy incursion, the political consequences could have been disastrous. Popular and political pressures therefore compelled him to scatter small armies around the perimeter at a couple of dozen places.

Davis's correspondence reflected these pressures. As the Confederate government prepared to move from Montgomery to Richmond and soldiers from various states began to concentrate in Virginia, telegrams and letters of protest cascaded across the president's desk. "The Gulf States expect your care, you were elected President of them, not of Virginia," complained an Alabamian. From the prominent Mississippian Jacob Thompson came a report that "the fear [here] is that [the] eye of the Administration is so exclusively fixed upon [Virginia] that we may be neglected & stripped of the means of defence." The Committee of Public Safety in Corpus Christi, Texas, pleaded for men and arms to repel a rumored Yankee invasion.[18] The son-in-law of Davis's brother Joseph wrote from his plantation in Louisiana that "there is great fear at present in this Country of an invasion down the river." The governor of Louisiana echoed this fear, and asked also for greater attention to the defense of Bayou Atchafalaya and Bayou Teche. "Much uneasiness felt here in consequence of our condition," declared the governor. "I am I may [say] constantly harassed on this subject. . . . Great opposition here to another man leaving the state, & I must say to a certain extent I participate in the feeling." Claiming to apprehend an attack on the Georgia coast, Governor Joseph Brown of that state expressed reluctance to send any more Georgia troops "to go glory hunting in Virginia. . . . While I still recognize the authority of the President . . . I demand the exercise of that authority in behalf of the defenseless and unprotected citizens of the State."[19]

Davis did his best to respond to those demands he considered reasonable, but there were not enough men and arms to satisfy all needs. To the governor of Tennessee he wrote that "your suggestion with regard to the distribution of the troops, in the several sections of Tennessee, is approved, and shall be observed, *so far as possible.*"[20] Brig. Gen. Joseph E. Johnston, the senior commander in Virginia, lamented the shortages of men and weapons to defend western Virginia. The governor backed

Johnston's complaints. "I wish I could send additional force to occupy Loudon," Davis told them, "but my means are short of the wants of each division of the wide frontier I am laboring to protect. . . . Our line of defence is a long one, and my duty embraces all its parts. . . . Missouri and Kentucky demand our attention, and the Southern coast needs additional defense."[21]

IN MAY 1861 THE CONFEDERATE GOVERNMENT ACCEPTED an invitation from Virginia to transfer the capital to Richmond. The accommodations at Montgomery were woefully inadequate, and moving the capital to Virginia would cement the vital allegiance of that state to the Confederacy. This action ensured that the most crucial operations of the war were likely to take place between the two capitals only one hundred miles apart. It presented Davis with the delicate task of balancing the defense of points distant from Richmond with the preeminent need to protect the capital. When the governors of South Carolina and Georgia petitioned for the return of their states' regiments from Virginia after the Union capture of the coastal islands of those states in the fall of 1861, Davis refused. "The threatening power before us [here] renders it out of the question that the troops specified should be withdrawn," he wrote. Davis instructed Secretary of War Judah P. Benjamin (who had replaced the hapless Leroy P. Walker) to reject the governors' entreaties. Benjamin bluntly told Brown that it would be "suicidal to comply with your request." Other governors were making

The Confederate executive mansion in Richmond

similar demands, and if the administration gave in to Brown it would have to give in to all of them. Confederate forces could not be broken into fragments "at the request of each Governor who may be alarmed for the safety of his people."[22]

Both the Union and Confederate governments organized their largest armies under what they presumed to be their best commanders to attack or defend the new Confederate capital. Twenty thousand Confederate troops under General Beauregard were stationed at Manassas Junction protecting this key railroad connection with Richmond to the south and the Shenandoah Valley to the west, where General Joseph Johnston commanded another twelve thousand defending the valley. Each Confederate force confronted a larger Union army, but interior lines utilizing the rail connection gave Southern armies the ability to reinforce one another more quickly than their adversaries could combine. Beauregard proposed to use this advantage by having Johnston join him at Manassas for an offensive to recapture Alexandria, which the Federals had seized in May. Davis rejected this suggestion, which would have abandoned the Shenandoah Valley to the enemy, who could then use the same rail network to attack Johnston and Beauregard from the rear while they were battling the main Union army in their front.[23]

Undeterred, Beauregard came up with an even more ambitious and fanciful scheme in July. Johnston should join him to attack the Yankees near Alexandria, and after defeating them the combined armies should return quickly to the valley, whip the enemy there, then move farther west to defeat the Federals in the mountains of western Virginia, where they had gained control of Unionist counties in that region. After these lightning strikes, the victorious Confederates could cross the Potomac and attack Washington. The exuberant Beauregard sent an aide, James Chesnut (whose wife, Mary Boykin Chesnut, kept a diary that became a famous source for Confederate history), to Richmond to present this plan to Davis. The president rose from a sickbed to meet with Chesnut and with Adj. Gen. Samuel Cooper and Gen. Robert E. Lee, who was serving as a military adviser to Davis. They heard Chesnut out, and gently but firmly rejected the proposal, which they described as impressive on paper and brilliant in results "if we should meet with no disaster in details"—a kind way of saying that it bore no relationship to the real world of logistics, transportation, and enemy actions.[24]

Davis did hope that if the enemy gave him sufficient time, he could build up an army in Virginia strong enough "to be able to change from the defensive to an offensive attitude" and "achieve a victory alike glorious and beneficial," to "drive the invader from Virginia & teach our insolent foe some lessons which will incline him to seek for a speedy peace."[25] These words offered a hint of what would become a hallmark of Davis's preferred military strategy during the next two years. He later labeled it "offensive-defensive"—the best way to defend the Confederacy was to seize opportunities to take the offensive and force the enemy to sue for peace.

But in July 1861 the enemy did not give him time and opportunity. A few days after disapproving of Beauregard's fantasy offensive, Davis learned of the Union army's advance toward

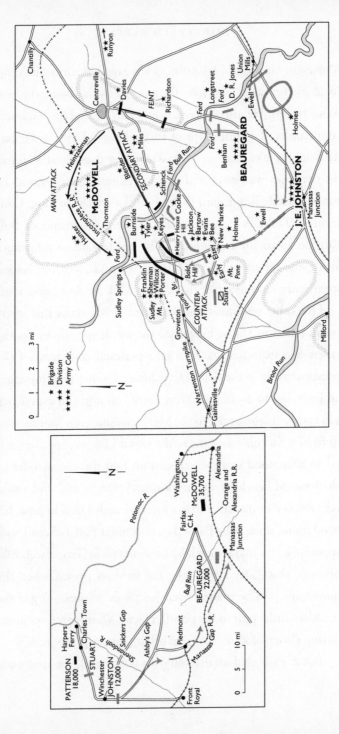

THE CAMPAIGN AND BATTLE OF FIRST MANASSAS, JULY 21, 1861

Manassas. He ordered Johnston to leave behind a small holding force in the valley and join Beauregard by rail with the rest of his troops. He also ordered Brig. Gen. Theophilus Holmes, commander of a contingent of three thousand men at Fredericksburg, to take them to Manassas.[26] This concentration using interior lines was successful. These reinforcements arrived in time to enable Beauregard to hold off the attacks by Brig. Gen. Irvin McDowell's Federals along the sluggish stream of Bull Run on a brutally hot July 21. The last brigade of Johnston's army, just off the train at Manassas in midafternoon, helped spearhead a counterattack that turned Union defeat into a rout.

One other reinforcement detrained at Manassas that afternoon: Jefferson Davis. Ever since the war began, many Southerners had expected Davis to take personal command of the principal army in the field. Davis himself sometimes intimated an intention to do so. His West Point training and experience as a combat commander in the Mexican-American War seemed to fit him for this role. One of the reasons for moving the capital to Richmond was the expectation that the commander in chief would be closer to the principal war theater and could take direct command.[27] After a meeting with Davis in June, his good friend since West Point days, Leonidas Polk (whom Davis appointed as a major general to command in Tennessee), told his wife that "Davis will take the field in person when the movement is to be made." Even Joseph E. Johnston urged the president to "appear in the position Genl. Washington occupied during the revolution. . . . Civil affairs can be postponed."[28]

But even if civil affairs could be postponed, the multitude

of tasks connected with organizing, arming, financing, and appointing commanders for armies scattered from Virginia to Texas required all of Davis's time and energy—and then some. He insisted on reading and acting on all of the papers that crossed his desk. He put in twelve to fourteen hours a day. This hands-on activity as commander in chief at his desk (or sickbed) left him little opportunity for hands-on command in the field. Nevertheless, as the prospect of battle in northern Virginia approached, he grew restless in Richmond and chafed to join the army concentrating at Manassas. The Confederate Congress was scheduled to meet in Richmond on July 20, however, and he needed to remain there to address it.

On the warm Sunday morning of July 21 he could stand it no longer. He commandeered a special train and with a single aide he chugged northward more than a hundred slow, frustrating miles. Arriving at Manassas Junction in midafternoon, Davis borrowed a horse and rode toward the sound of the guns. He was dismayed by what he first encountered: stragglers and wounded men bearing tales of defeat, damaged equipment, the usual detritus in the rear of a battlefield. Davis tried to rally the stragglers. "I am President Davis," he shouted. "Follow me back to the field." Some did. By the time Davis reached Johnston's headquarters, where he found the general sending reinforcements to the front, it was clear that the Confederates were victorious. Union troops were in headlong retreat. Davis rode farther forward and addressed the soldiers, who cheered him to the echo. It was perhaps his happiest moment in the war.[29]

Davis sent a jubilant telegram to Adjutant General Cooper

in Richmond: "Our forces have won a glorious victory. The enemy was routed and fled precipitately."[30] Johnston and Beauregard may have raised their eyebrows at this. Was the president trying to take credit for what they had achieved before he arrived? In any event, the three men were cordial with one another at Johnston's headquarters that evening. Davis wanted to organize a pursuit of the beaten enemy, and suggested that Beauregard or Johnston order such a movement. They remained silent, presumably because as commander in chief, Davis was now in charge. He began to dictate an order, but upon reflection and further consultation, he concluded that in the darkness and the disorganized confusion of even the triumphant Confederates, an effective pursuit was impossible. The next morning Beauregard ordered a reconnaissance forward, but heavy rain and empty haversacks with no immediate prospect of resupply brought the advance to a halt.[31]

In a private letter to Davis a few days later, General Johnston offered another reason for the army's inability to press after the enemy. "This victory disorganized our volunteers as utterly as a defeat would do in an army of regulars," Johnston reported. "Every body, officer and private, seemed to think he had fulfilled all his obligations to the country—& . . . it was his privilege to look after his friends, procure trophies, or amuse himself—It was several days after you left us [on July 23] before the regiments who had really fought could be reassembled. . . . This trait in the volunteer character gives us real anxiety."[32]

The failure to follow up the victory at Manassas with an effective pursuit stored up controversy for the future. But Confederates everywhere basked in the immediate afterglow of the battle. Davis promoted Beauregard from brigadier to full general (Johnston already held that rank). Beauregard's popularity, already great because of his capture of Fort Sumter, soared even higher. Davis returned to Richmond, and on the evening of July 23 he responded to the call of a large crowd outside his home for a speech. The diarist Mary Chesnut, a close friend of the president's, was untypically critical of his address. He "took all the credit to himself for the victory," she wrote. "Said the wounded roused & shouted for Jeff Davis—& the men rallied at the sight of him & rushed on & routed the enemy. The truth is Jeff Davis was not two miles from the battle-field—but he is greedy for military fame."[33]

Beauregard no doubt learned of this speech from James Chesnut, who had been his aide at the battle. The general began complaining about the failure of Commissary General Lucius B. Northrop to keep his army supplied; some of the regiments were nearly starving, reported Beauregard with considerable exaggeration. Northrop was noted as an old friend of Davis's from their army days together in the early 1830s, and Beauregard clearly intended his criticism of Northrop as an indictment of Davis's poor judgment in appointing him commissary general. Beauregard also began hinting to friendly congressmen that this supply deficiency was the reason he could not follow up the victory at Manassas. "The want of food and transportation has made us lose all the fruits of our victory," he told them. "From all accounts, Washington could have been taken up to the 24th instant, by twenty thousand men! Only think of the brilliant results we have lost by the two causes re-ferred to!"[34]

A dispute over army command injected additional poison into the deteriorating relationship between Davis and Beaure-gard. The latter's troops at Manassas (designated at the time as the Army of the Potomac—not to be confused with the Union army of the same name) had been merged with Johnston's army from the Shenandoah Valley, with Johnston as commander by seniority of rank. But Beauregard insisted on issuing orders to his own half of the army as if it were a separate organization. The new secretary of war, Judah Benjamin, tried to set him straight. "You are *second* in command of the *whole* Army of the Potomac, and not *first* in command of *half* of the army." Beau-regard was infuriated by Benjamin's lecturing style. He wrote to Davis asking him "as an educated soldier . . . to shield me from these ill-timed, unaccountable annoyances." Davis was getting fed up with Beauregard's complaints, and replied to him, "I do not feel competent to instruct Mr. Benjamin in the matter of style. . . . I cannot recognize the pretension . . . that your army and you are outside the limits of the law."[35]

This caustic correspondence took place in the midst of an-other contretemps between Davis and Beauregard. The general did not submit his official report of the Battle of Manassas until mid-October. For some reason never explained, the War De-partment did not forward a copy to Davis, who read an account of it in the *Richmond Dispatch*. This version focused on Beaure-gard's discussion of his plan for a multipronged offensive pre-sented by James Chesnut to Davis and Lee a week before the

P. G. T. Beauregard

battle, and their rejection of it. Beauregard implied that Davis had therefore prevented the glorious success that such an offensive was sure to have accomplished. Somehow the press accounts mixed up this issue with the question of why the army did not pursue the beaten Federals after Manassas. They concluded that Davis had restrained Beauregard (when the opposite was in fact the case). The president called for the actual report from the War Department. "With much surprise," he wrote Beauregard, "I found that the newspaper statements were sustained by the text of your report." The report itself, and especially its leak to the *Dispatch,* appeared to Davis like "an attempt to exalt yourself at my expense."[36] Indeed it was, and Davis never fully trusted Beauregard again. He also never fully put to rest the myth that he had prevented the Confederate army from capturing Washington in July 1861.[37]

This altercation with Beauregard was all the more painful for Davis because it came in the wake of a dispute with Joseph Johnston over his rank relative to other Confederate generals. In May 1861 the Confederate Congress had authorized the appointment of five full generals. The law specified that their rank would be equivalent to their relative grade in the United States Army in the same branch of the service before they had resigned to go south. Thus Davis gave the top ranking to Samuel Cooper as adjutant and inspector general, the same staff position he had held in the old army. Davis named his longtime friend Albert Sidney Johnston (who was on his way to Richmond from California) to the second position, followed by

Robert E. Lee, Joseph E. Johnston, and Pierre G. T. Beauregard. When Johnston learned in September of his number four grade, he exploded in anger. All along he had assumed that he was number one, based on his position as quartermaster general in the prewar army with the rank of brigadier general, while the three that Davis ranked above him had been colonels. Johnston sat down and wrote a blistering letter to Davis venting his outrage. The president's action, Johnston told him, was a "studied indignity" that tarnished "my fair fame as a soldier and a man" and was "a blow aimed at me only," especially since he was in command during the great victory at Manassas and those ranked above him had not "yet struck a blow for the Confederacy."[38]

This missive reached Davis while he was suffering another attack of illness, a recurrence of his old malarial fever, which no doubt sharpened the asperity of his reply. He acknowledged receiving Johnston's letter: "Its language is, as you say, unusual; its arguments and statements utterly one-sided; and its insinuations as unfounded as they are unbecoming."[39] That was it; no response to Johnston's arguments, no explanation of the reason for the ranking. Johnston's grade as a line officer in the old army was lieutenant colonel, while the three men ranked above him had been full colonels. His brigadier generalship was in a staff position, while his arm of service in the Confederacy was as a line officer, so under the terms of the law his prewar grade was below the others'. Even if Davis had bothered to explain all this to Johnston, the general would not have been satisfied. The insult to his honor, as he believed it to be, rankled him for the rest of his life. But he dropped the matter for now, and neither he nor Davis mentioned it to each other again.

After all, Davis and Johnston and Beauregard had a war to fight against the Yankees that was more important than a war among themselves. Their relations during strategy discussions that fall were professionally correct, if not warm. These discussions took place against the backdrop of a growing clamor from the press and public for an offensive. "The idea of waiting for blows, instead of striking them, is altogether unsuited to the genius of our people," declared the *Richmond Examiner.* "The aggressive policy is the truly defensive one. A column pushed forward into Ohio or Pennsylvania is worth more to us, as a defensive measure, than a whole tier of seacoast batteries from Norfolk to the Rio Grande."[40]

Davis agreed, for he too thought the best defense was a good offense. But he was also painfully aware of the shortages of arms and logistical capacity that precluded offensive operations in the fall of 1861. An anti-Davis faction centered on the *Examiner* and the *Charleston Mercury* began to form on this issue. The victory at Manassas, for which they credited Beauregard, convinced them that Confederate forces had the Yankees at their mercy and could go anywhere they liked. It was Davis, they charged, who held Beauregard back. "The continued attacks of the *Mercury,*" observed a South Carolina friend of the president's, "are making something of a party against him. . . . The policy which prevents forward movements by our army does not meet the approval of this party, and they, far removed from the seat of the war and ignorant of what reasons prevent a forward movement, deem themselves far more competent to judge of what is proper to be done than those who, bearing the brunt and seeing everything, are."[41]

Davis chafed at this censure. But "I have borne reproach in silence," he explained privately, "because to reply by an exact statement of facts would have exposed our weakness to the enemy." His critics, Davis added, "seem to have fallen into the not uncommon mistake of supposing that I have chosen to carry on the war upon a 'purely defensive' system." Nothing could be more wrong; "the advantage of selecting the time and place of attack was too apparent to have been overlooked." But there were not enough men and guns to take the offensive. "The country has supposed our armies more numerous than they were, and our munitions of war more extensive than they have been. . . . Without military stores, without the workshops to create them, without the power to import them, necessity not choice has compelled us to occupy strong positions and everywhere to confront the enemy without reserves."[42]

On September 30, 1861, Davis traveled from Richmond to the Confederate front lines near Centreville to confer with Johnston, Beauregard, and Maj. Gen. Gustavus W. Smith, a native Kentuckian who had recently committed to the Confederacy and was given a high position in the army. The four men met for several hours on October 1 to thrash out strategic options. The generals wanted to launch an offensive across the Potomac to flank Maj. Gen. George B. McClellan's Union Army of the Potomac out of its position at Alexandria and fight it in Maryland. Davis was all for the strategy. He had even brought maps of the Potomac fords. The president had been funneling newly organized regiments to the army; in the absence of strength reports from Johnston, he assumed that the army was substantially larger than it had been at Manassas. He was shocked to learn that, to the contrary, because of illness the number of effective troops was only about forty thousand.

Davis asked how many additional men would be necessary for the contemplated offensive. Another twenty thousand, the generals responded, and they must be well-trained troops, not raw recruits. Where would they come from? wondered the commander in chief as he reflected on his responsibility for the whole Confederacy, not just Virginia. From the southern Atlantic coast, from Pensacola, perhaps some from Tennessee, suggested Smith. "Can you not," he asked, "by stripping other points to the last they will bear, and, even risking defeat at all other places, put us in a condition to move forward? Success here at this time saves everything; defeat here loses all." No, he could not, answered Davis. He was already under fire from several governors for neglecting the defense of their states. To take more men from those states was impossible.[43]

The conference broke up on an unhappy note. There would be no Confederate offensive that fall. Nor would there be a Union offensive, for McClellan estimated Confederate strength at more than twice its actual numbers. Both armies went into winter quarters. And well before they emerged in the spring, the scene of action had shifted to the southern Atlantic coast and to the Tennessee and Cumberland Rivers in the West.

2.

WINTER OF
DISCONTENT

Jefferson Davis was born in Kentucky and returned there twice to attend school at St. Thomas College and Transylvania University before going on to West Point. Like his fellow Kentucky native Abraham Lincoln, the Confederate president was acutely aware of the state's strategic importance in the Civil War. Bordered by the Ohio and Mississippi Rivers, with the Cumberland and Tennessee Rivers flowing through it, Kentucky was both a buffer between North and South and a route of invasion. Heir to the nationalism of Henry Clay, the state had a pro-Confederate governor in 1861, but a majority of its legislature was Unionist. Divided in the allegiances of its people, Kentucky declared its neutrality at the beginning of the war and sought to mediate between the two sides. Davis and Lincoln both decided to respect this neutrality and refrained from sending troops into the state, for it was clear that whichever side did so first would drive the state into the arms of the other.

But pro-Confederate Kentuckians organized "state guard" regiments and Unionists formed "home guards." They were armed with weapons smuggled into the state, whose neutrality was becoming increasingly fragile. Confederate troops in Tennessee near the Kentucky border were commanded by Davis's longtime friend Maj. Gen. Leonidas Polk, who had left the United States Army after graduating from West Point to become an Episcopal priest and eventually a bishop. He donned a uniform again when the war began. Union troops at Cairo, Illinois, across the Ohio River from Kentucky, were commanded by Brig. Gen. Ulysses S. Grant. Fearing that Grant intended to seize the strategic heights overlooking the Mississippi River at Columbus, Kentucky, Polk decided to act first. He occupied Columbus on September 3, 1861.

Polk's fears were well founded and his movement was militarily sound. But it was a political blunder. Kentucky's legislature denounced the Confederate "invaders." The governor of Tennessee immediately wired Davis that Polk's action would "injure our cause" in Kentucky and urged the president to order Polk to withdraw his troops. Davis had the secretary of war send a withdrawal order, but this telegram crossed with one from Polk explaining the reasons for his action. In response, Davis became indecisive. He telegraphed Polk that "the necessity must justify the action," by which he may have meant that Polk should provide a fuller explanation before receiving presidential approval. But Polk interpreted the message itself as

Leonidas Polk

approval. He replied that Davis's telegram "gives great relief. The military necessity is fully verified and justified" by Grant's subsequent occupation of Paducah and Smithland in Kentucky, where the Tennessee and Cumberland Rivers flowed into the Ohio. Grant's action, of course, came in response to Polk's, and was endorsed by the Kentucky legislature. The governor of Tennessee continued to insist that the Confederate cause had suffered a setback in Kentucky, and most historians agree. But Davis came around to Polk's position that military necessity trumped political considerations.[1]

On September 15 Davis sent General Albert Sidney Johnston to take charge in Kentucky. His command embraced the Confederacy's largest military department, stretching from eastern Kentucky all the way across the Mississippi River to include Missouri and Arkansas. Confederate troops had invaded Missouri and had won the Battles of Wilson's Creek in August and Lexington in September. Although the official state governments of both Kentucky and Missouri remained loyal to the Union, pro-Confederate minorities established their own governments and were admitted to full representation in the Confederate Congress. But Union forces retained military and political control of most of both states during most of the war.

Five years older than Davis, Albert Sidney Johnston had been a mentor and friend when they both attended Transylvania University and the United States Military Academy in the 1820s. Johnston had remained Davis's idol ever since. Also a native of Kentucky, Johnston had become an adoptive Texan, fought in that republic's war of independence in 1836, and returned to the American army when Texas entered the Union. He was commanding the Department of the Pacific when the Civil War broke out. Johnston turned down a high command in the Union army, submitted his resignation, accepted a commission as the second-ranking full general in the Confederate army, made his way across the Southwest dodging Union patrols and Apache raiders, and in September arrived at Richmond, where Davis immediately assigned him to Kentucky.

Johnston made his headquarters at Bowling Green, from where he surveyed his huge department with despair. He had only forty thousand men to defend a line that stretched five hundred miles from the Cumberland Gap to southwest Missouri. Many of these men were raw recruits with inadequate arms and accoutrements. Johnston pleaded with Davis for reinforcements. In January 1862 he sent a staff officer to Richmond to appeal personally to Davis. The officer found the president "careworn and irritable" as he handed him a letter from Johnston suggesting that he strip other theaters to send men to Kentucky. "My God!" Davis exclaimed. "Why did General Johnston send you to me for arms and reinforcements, when he must know that I have neither. He has plenty of men in Tennessee, and they must have arms of some kind—shotguns, rifles, even pikes could be used." By the next day Davis had calmed down, but he still instructed the officer: "Tell my friend, General Johnston, that I can do nothing for him; that he must rely on his own resources."[2]

Although Johnston was short of men, he had plenty of ingenuity. He leaked disinformation that greatly puffed up the size of his army. These rumors and reports found their way into

Union lines, where they were swallowed without skepticism. The Union commander in Kentucky, Brig. Gen. William T. Sherman, expressed alarm at the reported buildup of Confederate forces. Sherman became so upset that the press began calling him insane, and he was replaced by Brig. Gen. Don Carlos Buell. Johnston managed gradually to increase his force and arm many of his men with better weapons than shotguns and pikes. He also received a significant reinforcement from Virginia: Pierre G. T. Beauregard, who had sought transfer from an unsatisfactory position as second in command to Joseph Johnston but was willing to accept the same position under Sidney Johnston. Davis was quite happy to see Beauregard leave Virginia.

Meanwhile, Grant had been preparing to attack Johnston's defenses at their most vulnerable points, Forts Henry and Donelson on the Tennessee and Cumberland Rivers just south of the Kentucky-Tennessee border. Union naval power on the rivers gave its army a considerable advantage over the Confederates, who had virtually no navy on these waters. On February 6 the Yankee river ironclads captured Fort Henry on the Tennessee River. Two "timberclad" gunboats steamed all the way up the river to the rapids at Florence, Alabama, wreaking much damage along the way. They burned the railroad bridge that connected Johnston's two main Kentucky forces at Columbus and Bowling Green, while Grant's army prepared to march against Fort Donelson on the Cumberland River.

The fall of Fort Henry shocked Davis into taking the previously rejected step of divesting the Gulf Coast of troops to reinforce Johnston. On February 8 orders went out to Maj. Gen.

Albert Sidney Johnston

Braxton Bragg at Pensacola and Maj. Gen. Mansfield Lovell at New Orleans to send seven or eight thousand men to Tennessee and Kentucky.[3] A few days later Davis ordered Bragg to abandon Pensacola (which the Federals then occupied) and go personally with the rest of his troops to Tennessee. He also ordered the river defense fleet of Confederate gunboats at New Orleans to go up the Mississippi River.[4] These actions enabled the Federals to capture New Orleans and gain control of the lower Mississippi River two months later—precisely the consequences Davis had warned against in his earlier refusals to concentrate most Confederate forces in Virginia and Tennessee.

None of these reinforcements would reach Sidney Johnston in time to save Fort Donelson and Nashville. In an emergency meeting at Bowling Green on February 7, Johnston, Beauregard, and their staffs canvassed their strategic options. The grandiloquent Beauregard proposed one of his fanciful schemes to concentrate all available Confederate troops to "smash" Grant's and Buell's armies in turn. Johnston rejected this idea. He wanted to give up Kentucky and retreat to the Nashville-Memphis line, leaving only a token force at Fort Donelson to delay Grant and concentrating the rest of the army to fight under more favorable conditions. But for some unexplained reason, Johnston changed his mind and decided to make a real stand at Fort Donelson— perhaps because its loss would lay Nashville open to the Union river navy. Instead of taking his whole force to Fort Donelson, however, he sent twelve thousand men (increasing the total garrison to seventeen thousand) and retreated with the rest to Nashville.

The first- and second-ranking commanders at Fort Donelson—John B. Floyd and Gideon Pillow—belonged to that fraternity known as "political generals." Floyd was a former governor of Virginia and secretary of war in the Buchanan administration; Pillow was a prominent Tennessee politician. Both Davis and Lincoln found it necessary as part of the mobilization of their polities for the war effort to appoint influential political leaders to military office. Some 30 percent of the general officers Davis named in 1861 belonged to this category.[5] It was the Confederacy's bad luck that two of them were in charge at Fort Donelson, where they faced two of the Union's best professionals, General Ulysses S. Grant and naval Flag Officer Andrew Hull Foote. After an ineffective defense, Floyd and Pillow fled the scene and left the lone Confederate professional, Brig. Gen. Simon Bolivar Buckner, to surrender thirteen thousand troops to Grant on February 16. Nashville fell a week later.

A shower of recriminations fell on the heads of Johnston and Davis. The Confederate Congress appointed an investigating committee. Tennessee's representatives and senators called for Johnston's removal. So did a delegation from the Tennessee legislature. To the latter, Davis responded: "If Sidney Johnston is not a general, we had better give up the war, for we have no general."[6] Privately, however, Davis admitted that the criticisms "have been painful to me, and injurious to us both . . . and damaged our cause." Attorney General Thomas Bragg noted that Davis "seems a good deal depressed—and though he holds up bravely, it is but too evident that he is greatly troubled."[7]

Johnston acknowledged in a letter to Davis that the loss of

Fort Donelson "was most disastrous and almost without remedy." He understood the reasons for the clamor against him, and implied a willingness to resign if Davis wished it. "The test of merit in my profession, with the people, is success," he acknowledged. "It is a hard rule, but I think it right." Davis replied with an expression of reassurance. "My confidence in you has never wavered," he told Johnston. "I hope the public will soon give me credit for judgment rather than continue to arraign me for obstinacy."[8] Davis showed no such magnanimity to Floyd and Pillow; he unceremoniously relieved them, and neither got another field command.[9]

The loss of Kentucky and much of Tennessee was not the full extent of Confederate woes in February 1862. A Union task force of warships and army brigades attacked and carried Roanoke Island, key to control of Pamlico and Albemarle Sounds in North Carolina. From there the Federals occupied much of the state's coastline, captured New Bern and Beaufort, and shut down all blockade running in and out of North Carolina ports except Wilmington. More than 2,500 Confederate soldiers surrendered at Roanoke Island. The son of Henry Wise, another influential political general, was killed in the battle there. North Carolinians had pleaded in vain with the Davis administration for more men and arms to defend their coast, but Secretary of War Judah Benjamin told them that he had none to send.

"Our President has lost the confidence of the country" was one of the milder comments of Virginia and North Carolina newspapers. "Davis's incapacity was lamentable," wrote the powerful Georgia politico and political general Robert Toombs,

KENTUCKY AND TENNESSEE, WINTER–SPRING 1862

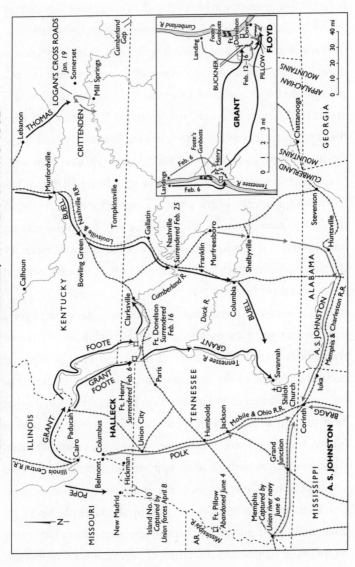

who had been a disappointed candidate for Davis's office a year earlier.[10] But most of the blame for the North Carolina defeats fell on Benjamin, who had been for months an unpopular secretary of war. Davis and Benjamin decided that the secretary should endure in silence the censure of a congressional investigating committee rather than reveal the Confederacy's weaknesses to the enemy by testifying to the lack of arms and men that had made it impossible to reinforce Roanoke Island. Benjamin resigned as secretary of war; Davis replaced him with Virginian George Wythe Randolph, a grandson of Thomas Jefferson and a veteran of the prewar United States Navy and of the Confederate army in 1861–62. He was a popular choice; less popular was Davis's appointment of Benjamin as secretary of state, a post in which he became one of the president's closest advisers and confidants.[11]

In the midst of these troubles, Davis was inaugurated for a full six-year term as president of the Confederate States of America on February 22. Until then he had been provisional president, elected by the same convention that created the Confederacy and adopted its Constitution a year earlier. Under that Constitution an election for president and Congress was held in November 1861. Davis and his vice-presidential running mate, Alexander H. Stephens, had no opposition in the election; most candidates for Congress also ran unopposed. This show of unity was misleading, however, and by the time of Davis's inauguration the seeds of an inchoate opposition were beginning to sprout as he became the target of reproach for Confederate setbacks.

Judah P. Benjamin

In his inaugural address, which he delivered outdoors in a pouring rain, the president took note of the altered mood of the public. "After a series of successes and victories, which covered our arms with glory, we have recently met with serious disasters," he acknowledged. But the same was true of their forebears in the American Revolution. Southerners must "renew such sacrifices as our fathers made to the holy cause of constitutional liberty. . . . To show ourselves worthy of the inheritance bequeathed to us by the patriots of the Revolution, we must emulate that heroic devotion which made reverses to them but the crucible in which their patriotism was refined." Although "the tide for the moment is against us, the final result in our favor is not doubtful. . . . It was, perhaps, in the ordination of Providence that we were to be taught the value of our liberties by the price which we pay for them."[12]

Eloquent and inspiring words, but could they be matched by deeds? Davis hoped that a change from the strategy of a dispersed defense to one of concentration would accomplish that purpose. "I acknowledge the error of my attempt to defend all of the frontier, seaboard and inland," he wrote privately. In a cabinet meeting on February 19, the president said that "the time had come for diminishing the extent of our lines—that we had not the men in the field to hold them and we must fall back."[13] Six days later Davis told Congress that "in the effort to protect by our arms the whole of the territory of the Confederate States" the government "had attempted more than it had power successfully to achieve." He announced that "strenuous efforts have been made to throw forward reinforcements" to the main armies in Mississippi and Virginia.[14]

Sidney Johnston was concentrating all of his forces at the rail junction of Corinth in northern Mississippi. There he faced a threat from Grant's army moving up the Tennessee River and Buell's army marching overland to join Grant in a combined thrust to capture Corinth. Polk received orders to abandon his huge fortifications at Columbus, Kentucky, and bring his men to Corinth. In Arkansas, Maj. Gen. Earl Van Dorn, who had fought and lost the Battle of Pea Ridge on March 7–8, also received orders to cross the Mississippi and join Johnston, abandoning Missouri and northern Arkansas to the enemy. Davis and Johnston intended to risk all on a counteroffensive to strike Grant at Pittsburg Landing on the Tennessee River, twenty miles from Corinth, before Buell could join him. It would be the Confederacy's first significant cast of the dice in a strategy of the offensive-defensive.[15]

After delays caused by the inexperience of the men and their officers, Johnston's forty thousand soldiers finally attacked Grant's thirty-five thousand on the morning of April 6 near a small log church called Shiloh. The initial Confederate assaults drove the unprepared Federals back with heavy losses to both sides. In midafternoon Johnston was hit in the leg by a bullet that severed an artery. He bled to death before his aides realized the seriousness of the wound. Beauregard took over and called a halt to the attack near dusk as Grant's final line stiffened and reinforcements from Buell's army began to arrive. That night

Beauregard sent a telegram to Davis announcing "a complete victory driving the enemy from every position." Davis's face no doubt lit up when he read these words, but his shoulders sagged as he reached the concluding line announcing Johnston's death. Nevertheless, the president sent Congress a message on April 8 informing it of a "glorious and decisive victory" and a retreating enemy.[16] Unknown to Davis at that moment, however, it was the Confederates who were retreating in disarray to Corinth after Grant and Buell counterattacked on April 7.

Davis was crushed by this news when it reached Richmond on April 10. Johnston's death turned out to have been in vain. Davis wept privately for the loss of his friend, which he pronounced "the greatest the country could suffer from. . . . The cause could have spared a whole State better than that great soldier."[17] To the end of his life Davis believed that Beauregard had snatched defeat from the jaws of victory by not pressing the attack on the evening of April 6—a conviction shared by some but not all modern historians of the battle.

In response to Beauregard's telegram announcing his retreat to Corinth, Davis uncharacteristically pushed the panic button. He wired the governors of South Carolina, Georgia, Alabama, Mississippi, and Louisiana to send all the men and arms they could spare to Beauregard "to meet the vast accumulation of the enemy before him." The governors scraped together a few thousand troops; Joseph Brown of Georgia also offered to send a thousand pikes and knives. Davis replied: "Pikes and knives will be acceptable. Please send them."[18]

Other reinforcements also reached Beauregard at Corinth, including nearly fifteen thousand men from Arkansas with General Earl Van Dorn, who had not arrived in time for the Battle of Shiloh. Beauregard vowed to hold Corinth "to the last extremity."[19] He faced a Union force composed of troops from the three armies of Grant, Buell, and Maj. Gen. John Pope, now united under the command of Maj. Gen. Henry W. Halleck, the senior Union officer in the Western theater. Halleck advanced at a snail's pace during May, threatening to envelop Corinth in a siege. Outnumbered almost two to one, with thousands of his troops on the sick list, Beauregard decided to pull out before he was surrounded. He did so skillfully on May 30, and retreated fifty miles south to Tupelo. Left isolated, with its rail connections to the east now severed, Memphis surrendered on June 6 to Union gunboats that had destroyed the Confederate Mississippi River fleet that day.

Beauregard wired Richmond that his "retreat was a most brilliant and successful one." Davis was shocked and disgusted by this "brilliant" flight. He compared Beauregard to a man "who can only walk a log when it is near the ground." He "has been placed too high for his mental strength, as he does not exhibit the ability manifested on smaller fields."[20] The president sent one of his aides, the son of deceased General Albert Sidney Johnston, with a series of written questions for Beauregard that signified his dissatisfaction with the general: Why did he not establish a stronger defensive position at Corinth? Why did he not attack the enemy's communications? How much equipment did he lose in the retreat? What were his plans for future operations, "and what prospect [is there] of the recovery of the territory that has been yielded?"[21]

Before he could receive any answers, Davis learned that Beauregard had taken a leave of absence from the army, without permission or even notification of the government. The general had been in ill health for months, and he obtained a surgeon's certification that he needed a rest of a week or ten days at a spa near Mobile. For Davis, this behavior was the last straw. He notified Beauregard that he was relieved of command and named Braxton Bragg as his successor.[22]

Beauregard got a much longer rest than he wanted. But because of the general's popularity among segments of the press and public, Davis knew that he could not keep him on the shelf indefinitely. In September he gave Beauregard command of the defenses of Charleston, where he did an effective job of warding off Union attacks during the next year and a half. Beauregard remained bitter toward the president, however, calling him (in private) a "living specimen of gall & hatred . . . either demented or a traitor to his high trust. . . . If he were to die to-day, the whole country would rejoice at it, whereas, I believe, if the same thing were to happen to me, they would regret it."[23]

THESE REVERSES IN THE WINTER AND SPRING OF 1862 CAME in the midst of a crisis in army organization and recruitment. About half of all Confederate soldiers had enlisted for one year in 1861—despite Davis's urging that Congress require three-year commitments. Their times would begin to expire in early 1862, creating the prospect that the armies would melt away just as the Yankees were advancing on all fronts. Congress tried to address this issue in December 1861 with a law offering one-year men who reenlisted a fifty-dollar bounty, a sixty-day furlough, and the opportunity to join new regiments and elect new officers if they did not like their old ones. This remedy was worse than the disease; it promised to disrupt the organization of many regiments more than expiring enlistments would have done. The various Southern states also had conflicting provisions for their militias, which created confusion when these troops were called into Confederate service. And in any case, few one-year men seemed to be reenlisting.

By March 1862 the new secretary of war, George W. Randolph; General Robert E. Lee, who had just returned from a four-month stint commanding defenses on the southern Atlantic coast; and Davis himself had become convinced that conscription was the only feasible solution. Randolph drew up legislation for this purpose; on March 28 Davis sent Congress a special message recommending the adoption of a measure making all white male citizens eighteen to thirty-five years old eligible to be drafted for three years. Davis initially opposed a provision requiring one-year men to serve for two more years; this would be a breach of contract, he argued. But Randolph convinced the president that this requirement was a military necessity, and Davis finally came around.

Opponents in Congress contended that conscription was a form of tyranny and coercion that Southern states had seceded to escape. But an overwhelming majority of the Senate and two-thirds of the House agreed with Senator Louis Wigfall of Texas, who warned his colleagues to "cease this child's play. . . . The enemy are in some portions of almost every State in the Confederacy. . . . We need a large army. How are you going to get it? . . . No man has any individual rights, which come into conflict with the welfare of the country." Davis signed the bill into law on April 16.[24]

The conscription law had some loopholes that stored up troubles for its enforcement: exemptions for some occupations crucial to war production (and some that were not); a provision that allowed a drafted man to hire a substitute; and confusion about which categories of state government officials and militia officers were exempt. Many of these issues would cross Davis's desk in the next three years and cause him numerous headaches. The first—and most persistent—of those headaches was Governor Joseph Brown of Georgia, who denounced the draft as a "dangerous usurpation by Congress of the reserved rights of the States" and said that it was "at war with all the principles for which Georgia entered into the revolution."[25]

Davis plowed through Brown's pamphlet-length letters condemning conscription and patiently replied, also at considerable length. The president explained the constitutional power of the Confederate government to draft men into the army. The Constitution authorized the government "to raise and support armies" and "to provide for the common defence." It also contained another clause (likewise copied from the United States

Constitution) empowering Congress to make all laws "necessary and proper for carrying into execution the foregoing powers." No one could doubt the necessity, wrote Davis, "when our very existence is threatened by armies vastly superior in numbers. . . . Congress has exercised only a plainly granted specific power in raising its armies by conscription. I cannot share the alarm and concern about State rights which you so evidently feel, but which seem to me quite unfounded."[26]

Brown remained unconvinced and unmollified. He continued to be a thorn in Davis's side. But Georgia also sent its full quota of troops, and perhaps more, into Confederate armies. Meanwhile, another issue raised its head and furnished fodder for a nascent opposition to the Davis administration's "despotic" violation of civil liberties. This matter became an embarrassment for Davis. In his inaugural address on February 22, he had contrasted the Confederacy's refusal "to impair personal liberty or the freedom of speech, of thought, or of the press" with Lincoln's suspension of the writ of habeas corpus and imprisonment without trial of "civil officers, peaceful citizens, and gentlewomen" in vile "Bastilles."[27] Davis overlooked the suppression of civil liberties in parts of the Confederacy, especially East Tennessee, where several hundred Unionists languished in Southern "Bastilles." Five days after Davis's inaugural address, Congress authorized him to suspend the writ of habeas corpus in areas that were in "danger of attack by the enemy."[28]

Davis promptly declared martial law in several places, including Richmond. Provost marshals enforced a requirement of passes for travel, banned sales of liquor, and jailed several "disloyal" citizens, including two women and John Minor Botts, a prominent Virginia Unionist and former United States congressman. At the same time, however, Davis did curb the excessive enforcement of such measures by some of his generals who commanded military departments. And unlike Lincoln, who suspended the writ on his own authority, Davis acted only when Congress authorized him to do so—for a total of seventeen months on three different occasions during the war. Nevertheless, the leading historian of civil liberties during the Civil War, Mark Neely, has found records of four thousand political prisoners in the Confederacy. The records are incomplete, and there were surely several thousand more. "Abraham Lincoln and Jefferson Davis acted alike as commanders in chief when it came to the rights of the civilian populace," Neely concluded. "Both showed little sincere interest in constitutional restrictions on government authority in wartime. Both were obsessed with winning the war."[29]

For Davis that obsession took on a sharper edge as the Confederacy seemed to be losing the war in the West and along its coastline and rivers. Even in Virginia the outlook was dire in early 1862. "Events have cast on our arms and our hopes the gloomiest shadows," Davis lamented to General Joseph E. Johnston in February.[30] The president summoned Johnston to a strategy conference with cabinet members on February 19 and 20. For many hours they discussed the vulnerability of Johnston's army at Centreville to a flanking movement by McClellan's large force via the Occoquan or Rappahannock River. They agreed that Johnston should pull back to a more defensible position south of the Rappahannock. But the wretched condition of roads caused by winter rains and the chaotic state of the railroads made a quick withdrawal impossible. Davis ordered Johnston to send his large guns, camp equipage, and huge stockpiles of meat and other supplies southward as transportation became available, and to prepare to retreat with the army when he received definite orders.

In early March, however, Johnston began a precipitate withdrawal when his scouts detected Federal activity that he thought was the beginning of McClellan's flanking movement. Without informing Richmond (he feared a leak), Johnston fell back so quickly that he was compelled to leave behind or destroy his heavy guns, ammunition, and mounds of supplies, including 750 tons of meat and other foodstuffs. In Richmond Davis heard rumors of this destruction and retreat, but as he later told the general, "I was at a loss to believe it." When he finally heard the truth from Johnston on March 15, the president's distress at the losses the Confederacy could ill afford was acute.[31]

Davis's confidence in Johnston had been waning for some time. As things went from bad to worse during February and March, the president decided to recall Robert E. Lee from the southern Atlantic coast to become general-in-chief of all

Joseph E. Johnston

Confederate armies.[32] Davis and Lee had known each other since their days at West Point (Davis graduated one year ahead of Lee). They had worked together cordially in the early months of the war when Lee served as a military adviser to the president after the government moved to Richmond. Davis used Lee as a sort of troubleshooter, sending him in July 1861 to western Virginia to regain control of the region from Union forces, and to South Carolina in November to reorganize coastal defense. For reasons largely beyond his control, Lee had failed to accomplish much in what became West Virginia and had met with partial success along the southern Atlantic coast only by withdrawing Confederate defenses inland beyond reach of Union gunboats.

Despite this mixed record, Davis retained his faith in Lee's abilities and wanted him by his side. The president had his congressional allies introduce a bill to create the position of "Commanding General of the Armies of the Confederate States," intending to name Lee to the post. But Davis's critics in Congress, who blamed him for Confederate reverses, amended the bill to enable the "commanding general" to take direct control of any army in the field without authorization from the president. Davis believed that this provision would usurp his constitutional powers as commander in chief, and he vetoed the bill on March 14. A day earlier he had issued an order assigning Lee to duty in Richmond and charging him "with the conduct of military operations . . . under the direction of the President."[33]

Lee's first task was to help Davis decide what to do about the situation in Virginia. From his desk in Richmond, Lee instructed Maj. Gen. Thomas J. "Stonewall" Jackson to make diversionary attacks with his small army in the Shenandoah Valley to prevent the Federals from concentrating all of their troops against Richmond. During the next two months Jackson carried out these orders in spectacular fashion. Meanwhile, McClellan's army began landing near Fort Monroe at the tip of the peninsula in Virginia formed by the James and York Rivers, seventy miles southeast of Richmond. When the Federals advanced toward the Confederate defenses held by Maj. Gen. John B. Magruder's twelve thousand troops, Davis and Lee ordered Johnston to send part of his army from the Rappahannock to Magruder. As the Union buildup continued, they instructed him to bring his whole army to the peninsula. Johnston proceeded to do so, but after inspecting Magruder's line at Yorktown, he recommended that the Confederates withdraw all the way back to Richmond, concentrate the Virginia forces there, and strip the Carolinas and Georgia of troops to fight the decisive battle of the war at Richmond. Winning there, they could then reoccupy the regions temporarily yielded to the enemy.

Here was a bold suggestion for a high-risk strategy of concentration for an offensive-defensive of the kind later associated with Lee. But on this occasion Lee opposed the idea. In an all-day meeting of Davis, Lee, Johnston, and Secretary of War Randolph on April 14, Lee and Johnston discussed the matter at great length. Lee argued for making the fight at Yorktown, where the big guns at the Gloucester Narrows on the York River and the CSS *Virginia* on the James River would protect the army's flanks. An old navy man, Randolph pointed out that pulling back from Yorktown would mean abandoning Norfolk with its Gosport Navy Yard, where the *Virginia* had been rebuilt from the captured USS *Merrimack*. Davis listened carefully to the arguments, took an active part in the discussion, and finally decided in Lee's and Randolph's favor. The Confederates would make their stand at Yorktown, where Johnston took command of 60,000 troops facing McClellan with 110,000.[34]

Instead of attacking, McClellan dug in his siege artillery and prepared to pulverize the Confederate defenses. This preparation continued for several weeks while the armies skirmished but did little damage to each other. Despite having been overruled by Davis, Johnston still intended to evacuate the Yorktown line without a fight. He delayed that move until McClellan was ready to open with his heavy artillery. Johnston failed to keep Davis and Lee informed of his intention until the last minute on May 1, when he told the president that he must pull out the next night. Davis was shocked. He replied that such a sudden retreat would mean the loss of Norfolk and possibly of the *Virginia* and other ships under construction there. Johnston consented to wait—for one more day. On the night of May 3–4 his army stealthily left the Yorktown line and began a retreat toward Richmond. The Confederates fought a rearguard battle with the cautiously pursuing Federals at Williamsburg, and continued to a new line behind the Chickahominy River twenty miles from Richmond. Norfolk fell to the enemy, and the

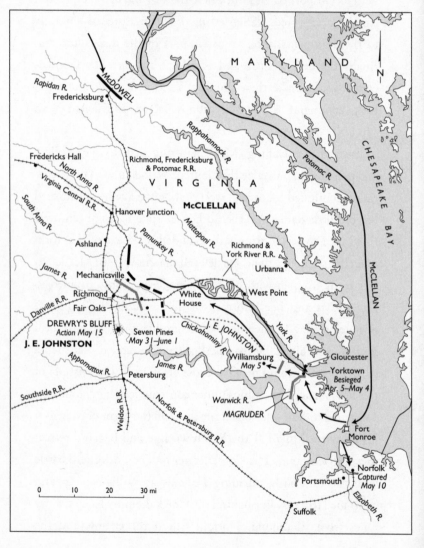

THE PENINSULA CAMPAIGN,
APRIL–JUNE 1862

Virginia's crew had to blow her up because her draft was too great to get up the James River.[35]

Davis was dismayed by these developments. A congressman reported that he found the president "greatly depressed in spirits." Davis's niece from Mississippi was visiting the Confederate White House at the time. She wrote to her mother that "Uncle Jeff. is miserable. . . . Our reverses distressed him so much. . . . Everybody looks drooping and sinking. . . . I am ready to sink with despair."[36] Davis and several cabinet members sent their families away from Richmond for safety. The secretary of war boxed up his archives ready for shipment before the capital fell. The Treasury Department loaded its specie reserves on a special train that kept steam up for an immediate departure.[37]

Davis allowed his anguish to leak into a letter to Johnston lamenting "the drooping cause of our country." The ostensible purpose of the letter was to prod Johnston into carrying out Davis's orders to group regiments from the same state together in brigades as a boost to morale. "Some have expressed surprise at my patience with you when orders to you were not observed," the president told his general. Johnston recognized this rebuke for what it was, an expression of exasperation with Johnston's conduct of the campaign. If he had received such a letter from someone who could be "held to personal accountability," Johnston told his wife, he would have challenged him to a duel.[38]

In this time of troubles, Davis turned to religion. He had been attending St. Paul's Episcopal Church in Richmond and had grown friendly with its rector, the Reverend Charles Minnigerode. Davis could not remember whether he had been baptized as a child, so he asked Minnigerode to baptize him and confirm him as a member of the church on May 6.[39] One of Davis's newspaper tormentors, the *Richmond Examiner,* waxed sarcastic about this event: "When we find the President standing in a corner telling his beads, and relying on a miracle to save the country, instead of mounting his horse and putting forth every power of the Government to defeat the enemy, the effect is depressing in the extreme."[40]

But Davis was in fact mounting his horse and exerting all of his energy to try to defeat the enemy. A fine horseman, Davis was in the habit of riding out in the afternoon for exercise and diversion. He used these occasions to visit army headquarters on the Chickahominy and the batteries placed at Drewry's Bluff on the James River seven miles from Richmond to stop the Union navy. Those guns did indeed drive back Northern warships, including the *Monitor,* on May 15, saving Richmond from the fate of New Orleans three weeks earlier, when the city had surrendered with naval guns trained on its streets.

But Richmond still seemed in great danger from General McClellan's large army approaching the capital at a snail's pace. Although Johnston chose not to reveal his plans to Davis (or Lee), the president expected him to defend the line of the Chickahominy and even to launch a counterattack if he stopped McClellan along that sluggish stream. Davis still had not lost entire faith in Johnston, despite his previous disappointments. "As on all former occasions," he told the general on May 17, "my design is to suggest not to direct, recognizing the impossibility of any one to decide in advance and reposing confidently as well on your ability as your zeal it is my wish to leave you with the fullest powers to exercise your judgment."[41]

Unknown to Davis, Johnston had already decided to withdraw to a new position just three or four miles east of Richmond. When the president rode out the next day to visit Johnston on the Chickahominy, he was taken aback when he encountered the army before he had ridden more than a few miles. Davis confronted Johnston and asked why he had pulled back so close to the capital. The general replied that the ground was so swampy and the drinking water so bad in the Chickahominy lowlands that he had moved to better ground and a safer supply of water. Davis was unnerved. Do you intend to give up Richmond without a battle? he asked. Johnston's reply was equivocal. The president responded with asperity. He told Johnston, according to one of Davis's aides who was present, "that if he was not going to give battle, he would appoint someone to the command who would."[42]

Davis rode back to Richmond and summoned his cabinet and General Lee to a meeting the following day. He also asked Johnston to attend, so that everyone could learn his intentions. The afternoon of the meeting, Davis wrote to his wife: "I have been waiting all day for [Johnston] to communicate his plans. . . . We are uncertain of everything except that a battle must be near at hand."[43] Johnston never showed up, but Davis went ahead with the conference, where he expressed his anxiety about the fate of Richmond. According to Postmaster General John Reagan, Lee became emotional. "Richmond must not be given up," he declared. "It shall not be given up." As Lee spoke, Reagan recalled, "tears ran down his cheeks. I have seen him on many occasions and at times when the very fate of the Confederacy hung in the balance, but I never saw him show equally deep emotion."[44]

The next day Davis assured a delegation from the Virginia legislature that Richmond would indeed be defended. "A thrill of joy electrifies every heart," wrote the diary-keeping War Department clerk John B. Jones. "A smile of triumph is on every lip."[45] Johnston finally seemed to get the message. He discovered that McClellan had crossed to the southwest bank of the Chickahominy with part of his army, leaving the rest on the other side. Johnston informed Lee that he intended to cross the stream with three divisions and attack the force on the northeast bank on May 22. Davis had earlier discussed precisely such a tactical operation with Lee, so he approved Johnston's plan. On the twenty-second the president rode out to the bluff overlooking the Chickahominy, then down to the river itself, to "see the action commence," as he wrote to his wife. But he found nothing happening and no one to tell him why the attack had been called off. Only later did General Gustavus Smith, whose division was to lead the attack, tell Davis that a local citizen had informed him that the enemy was strongly posted behind Beaver Dam Creek, so he had decided not to attack. This was not the first time that Smith had frozen under pressure. Davis was disconsolate. "Thus ended the offensive-defensive programme," he wrote, "from which Lee expected much, and of which I was hopeful."[46]

Almost the same scenario repeated itself exactly a week later, on May 29. Once again Johnston planned to attack McClellan's right flank north of the Chickahominy, and once again he called it off without informing Davis. The president discovered the cancellation only after riding out to the river on another futile mission.[47] Johnston had changed his mind and decided to assault the two corps south of the Chickahominy and nearest Richmond. The general later explained that he did not tell Davis of this change "because it seemed to me that to do so would be to transfer my responsibilities to his shoulders. I could not consult him without adopting the course he might advise, so that to ask his advice would have been, in my opinion, to ask him to command for me."[48]

Johnston's peculiar notion of the correct relationship with his commander in chief meant that Davis first learned of the general's changed plan of attack when he heard artillery firing on the afternoon of May 31. He quickly left his office, mounted his horse, and rode toward the sound of the guns. When he arrived near the village of Seven Pines (which gave its name to the battle), he saw Johnston riding away toward the front. Davis's aides were convinced that the general left to avoid the president. The battle was going badly for the Confederates. Maj. Gen. James Longstreet's division had taken the wrong road and blocked the advance of other divisions. The attack started late, and although it initially succeeded in routing one Union corps, reinforcements streamed across an almost flooded bridge over the Chickahominy and drove the Confederates back.

Davis came under artillery and musket fire as he and his

aides tried to rally retreating soldiers. A reporter for a Memphis newspaper described the president "sitting on his 'battle horse' immediately behind our line of battle. . . . I was much struck with the calm, impassive expression of his countenance and his proud bearing as he sat erect and motionless, intently gazing at the enemy. . . . Bullets whistled plentifully around, but he never bootled his eye for them."[49]

Davis issued orders and sent couriers for reinforcements, but as dusk approached it was clear that the Confederate attack had ground to a halt. At that moment, stretcher bearers passed the president's party carrying a seriously wounded Johnston to the rear. All animosity forgotten, Davis rushed to Johnston's side and spoke to him with genuine concern. "The old fellow bore his suffering most heroically," Davis wrote to his wife. It was obvious that Johnston would be out of action for several months. As Davis and Lee rode together back to Richmond that night, the president told him that he was now the commander of what Lee would soon designate the Army of Northern Virginia. A new era would dawn with that army's new name and new commander. "God will I trust give us wisdom to see and valor to execute the measures necessary to vindicate the just cause," wrote Davis as he entered into his new command relationship with Lee.[50]

3.

WAR SO GIGANTIC

Although Confederate armies were driven back on all fronts in the spring of 1862, some voices continued to call for an invasion of the North. Even as the War Department and Treasury Department packed archives and gold reserves for possible evacuation, the *Richmond Dispatch* declared that the public favored "an advance into the enemy's territory. Will the voice of the people again be denied?" The *Charleston Mercury* denounced the government's "defensive policy" and urged that "two powerful columns . . . be put in motion toward the banks of the Ohio and the Susquehanna."[1] Governor Joseph Brown of Georgia, normally insistent on retaining troops for local protection, unexpectedly offered Davis men from the state's coastal defenses to help form an army "to liberate Tennessee, penetrate Kentucky, and menace Cincinnati. . . . Let us invade their Territory, and fight where there are plenty of provisions." Virtually besieged in Richmond, Davis no doubt considered these entreaties delusional. But he thanked Brown for the offer, assured him that "such campaign as you suggest has long been desired," and that "its adoption is a question of power, not of will."[2]

With a like-minded general now in command of the newly named Army of Northern Virginia, Davis could contemplate at least a limited offensive to relieve the threat to Richmond. Stonewall Jackson's operations in the Shenandoah Valley had temporarily reduced enemy pressure from that direction. Lee proposed to reinforce Jackson for a raid into Maryland and possibly even Pennsylvania, which he hoped "would call all the enemy from our Southern coast & liberate those states." Davis concurred, and sent three brigades toward the valley. But even with these reinforcements Jackson would not be strong enough for a real invasion. Lee decided instead to carry out a plan originally suggested by Davis to bring Jackson from the valley to combine with Lee in a strike against the Union flank and rear north of the Chickahominy—similar to Johnston's aborted maneuvers on May 22 and 29, with the added factor of Jackson's cooperation.[3]

Brig. Gen. J. E. B. Stuart's famous cavalry expedition that resulted in a ride completely around the Army of the Potomac (June 12–15) revealed that McClellan's right flank was vulnerable to such an attack. To enable part of the Army of Northern Virginia to hold the line south of the Chickahominy so that the rest could take part in the flank attack, Lee ordered his troops to dig miles of trenches and build formidable earthworks. Complaining that they had enlisted to fight and not to work like slaves (in fact, actual slaves did much of this work), many soldiers and their allies in the press derisively labeled Lee the "King of Spades."

Davis fully backed his general. He deplored the "politicians, newspapers, and uneducated officers" who "created such a prejudice in our army against labor that it will be difficult until taught by sad experience to induce our troops to work efficiently. " McClellan was digging his way toward Richmond, noted Davis, and Confederates must neutralize his works. "If we succeed in rendering his works useless," Davis explained to his wife, who was in North Carolina, "I will endeavor by movements which are not without great hazard to countervail the Enemys policy" by attacking his open flank. "I have much confidence in our ability to give him a complete defeat, and then it may be possible to teach him the pains of invasion and to feed our army on his territory."[4]

A skirmish south of the Chickahominy provoked by a Union reconnaissance on June 25 became, in retrospect, the first of what was subsequently named the Seven Days' Battles. The following day Lee put in motion the operations north of the river to attack the enemy flank at Beaver Dam Creek. Once again the commander in chief rode out to observe his army in battle; once again it began to appear that there would be no battle. Lee's plan called for Maj. Gen. A. P. Hill's division to attack when Jackson notified Hill that he was in position on the Union flank. As the hours ticked away, the silence grew oppressive among the Confederate officers with Lee and Davis waiting for the action to begin. In late afternoon Hill's guns finally opened up, but Lee soon learned that Jackson was nowhere to be found, and Hill had grown tired of waiting. Slowed by felled trees over the roads, faulty maps, and the fatigue of his men and himself, Jackson was miles away.

Once Hill went in, it was too late to call off an attack that seemed headed toward bloody failure. Irritated and embarrassed, Lee noticed that Davis and an entourage that included aides, assorted politicians, and the secretaries of war and the navy had come under enemy artillery fire. Lee rode over to Davis and asked, with an edge to his voice, "Who are all this army of people, and what are they doing here?" Taken aback, Davis replied: "It is not my army, General." "It is certainly not my army, Mr. President," Lee responded, "and this is no place for it. . . . Any exposure of a life like yours is wrong." Davis said meekly, "Well General, if I withdraw, perhaps they will follow me." Suiting action to words, Davis turned his horse and moved away. As he did so, a soldier nearby was killed by an enemy shell. Davis rode only as far as a line of bushes along a stream that concealed him from Lee, then stopped, still within range of Union guns, to watch the backwash of Hill's attack, which was repulsed with heavy loss by Federals dug in behind Beaver Dam Creek.[5]

Having won this round, McClellan decided to pull back his thirty thousand men north of the Chickahominy several miles to a new line behind Boatswain's Swamp near Gaines' Mill. Lee followed and launched a full-scale attack with fifty-five thousand men on June 27, this time including Jackson's troops. After a series of failed assaults, the Confederates finally broke the

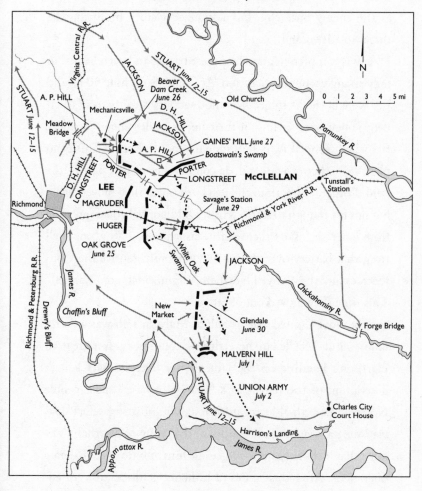

THE SEVEN DAYS' BATTLES,
JUNE 25–JULY 1, 1862

enemy line toward dusk. The Federals again retreated, this time heading for a new base on the James River. Lee attacked repeatedly, at Savage's Station on June 29, Glendale on June 30, and Malvern Hill on July 1, losing twice as many killed and wounded as the enemy but achieving a strategic victory by lifting the threat to Richmond.

Davis was present at each of these battles and even helped to rally stragglers on one occasion. At Glendale on June 30 he and Lee were both the subjects of another "Davis to the rear" incident. They were sitting on their horses under enemy artillery fire when General A. P. Hill rode up and declared: "This is no place for either of you, and, as commander of this part of the field, I order you both to the rear." Abashed, they moved back, but not far enough to satisfy Hill. "Did I not tell you to go away from here?" he asked them with exasperation. "Why, one shell from that battery over yonder may presently deprive the Confederacy and the Army of Northern Virginia of its commander!" This time they moved out of range.[6]

The final Confederate assault at Malvern Hill was a costly failure. But McClellan nevertheless continued his retreat to Harrison's Landing on the James River. Despite McClellan's description of the retreat as a "change of base," most people North and South alike regarded it as a humiliating defeat. Davis issued a congratulatory order to the Army of Northern Virginia that included a none-too-subtle hint of future Confederate operations. After this "series of brilliant victories" over an enemy "vastly superior to you in numbers and in the material of war," proclaimed the president, you will move on to "your one great object . . . to drive the invader from your soil, and carrying your standards beyond the outer bounds of the Confederacy, to wring from an unscrupulous foe the recognition of your birthright, community independence."[7]

Davis gave private assurances that he meant what he said publicly. He agreed with critics who maintained that the ultimate consequence of purely defensive war was surrender. "There could be no difference of opinion as to the advantage of invading over being invaded," he told John Forsyth, the mayor of Mobile and editor of the influential *Mobile Register*. However, "the time and place for invasion has been a question not of will but of power." Davis reiterated that he had silently endured criticism of the defensive strategy during the earlier shortage of men and arms, "because to correct the error would have required the disclosure of facts which the public interest demanded should not be revealed." But now, with a victorious army in Virginia and captures of weapons that ended the arms famine, the country could soon look for offensive operations. General Lee "is fully alive to the advantage of the present opportunity, and will, I am sure, cordially sustain and boldly execute my wishes to the full extent of his power."[8]

Lee was if anything more offensive-minded than Davis. He did indeed intend to act "boldly." Retaining part of his army to watch the idle Federals at Harrison's Landing, Lee sent Jackson to confront the newly formed Union Army of Virginia under General John Pope moving against Richmond from the north. "We hope soon to strike another blow here," Davis explained to one of his Western generals, "and are making every effort to

Robert E. Lee

increase the force so as to hold one army in check whilst we strike the other."[9] Jackson defeated part of Pope's army at Cedar Mountain on August 9. When McClellan began to evacuate the peninsula to reinforce Pope's army, Lee and Longstreet joined Jackson to assail Pope before McClellan's men could join him. Davis stripped the Richmond defenses of veteran troops to bolster Lee's force, leaving only raw recruits in the capital. "Confidence in you," Davis telegraphed to Lee as he forwarded two full divisions to him, "overcomes the view that would otherwise be taken of the exposed condition of Richmond."[10]

Lee fully justified this confidence with a notable victory at the Battle of Second Manassas on August 29–30. Pope's beaten army retreated into the Washington defenses, opening Maryland to the invasion that Davis had long wanted to undertake. Lee acknowledged to Davis that his army was "not properly equipped for an invasion of an enemy's territory. It lacks much of the material of war, is feeble in transportation, the animals being much reduced, and the men poorly provided with clothes, and in thousands of instances, are destitute of shoes." Nevertheless, "we cannot afford to be idle, and though weaker than our opponents in men and military equipments, must endeavor to harass, if we cannot destroy them. . . . The movement is attended with much risk, yet I do not consider success impossible."[11]

Neither did Davis, who recognized the political and diplomatic as well as military potential of the invasion. Northern "Copperhead" Democrats were denouncing the war as a failure and calling for peace negotiations. Upcoming Northern congressional elections might result in a Democratic takeover of the House of Representatives. "Liberation" of Maryland and its adherence to the Confederacy seemed possible. Davis was aware of the British and French desire for an end of the war and of the Union blockade that had drastically reduced imports of cotton and thrown thousands of their textile workers out of employment. Davis and Lee were avid readers of Northern newspapers smuggled across the lines. These papers were full of information about political unrest and diplomatic maneuvers that might lead to foreign recognition of the Confederacy. A successful invasion of Maryland and another victory over the Army of the Potomac might accomplish these ends. "The present posture of affairs," Lee wrote to Davis on September 8, four days after he had crossed the Potomac into Maryland, "places it in our power . . . to propose [to the Union government] . . . the recognition of our independence." Such a proposal, "coming when it is in our power to inflict injury on our adversary . . . would enable the people of the United States to determine at their coming elections whether they will support those who favor a prolongation of the war, or those who wish to bring it to a termination."[12]

Davis intended to join Lee in Maryland to exploit these possibilities and to be present at the anticipated battle as he had been at those near Richmond. Fearing the danger of capture by roving Union cavalry, and probably not wanting Davis looking over his shoulder, Lee discouraged the president from coming. Davis nevertheless departed from Richmond on September 7 with a former governor of Maryland in tow, hoping to use his influence to attract Marylanders to the Confederacy. They got

LEE'S INVASION OF MARYLAND, SEPTEMBER 1862

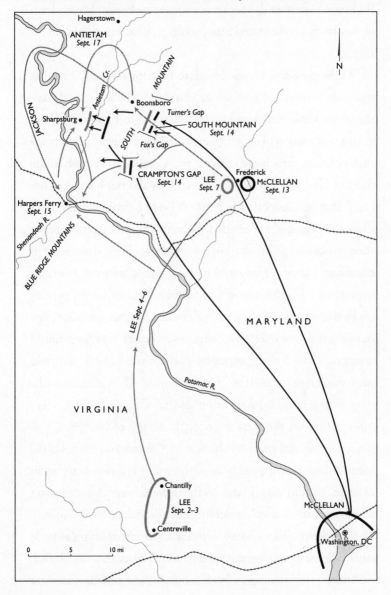

only as far as Warrenton, Virginia, and returned from there to Richmond the next day for reasons never explained. Davis's fragile health had been giving him problems, which may explain his return.

As the president traveled back to his capital, Lee's army was traveling in several directions in Maryland. Having cut the Baltimore & Ohio Railroad between Washington and the Union garrison at Harpers Ferry, Lee expected the Federals to evacuate that position, which lay athwart the Confederate supply route from the Shenandoah Valley. When they did not leave, Lee decided that he must capture Harpers Ferry before he could continue the invasion. He divided the army into five parts, three of them to converge on the enemy garrison. They succeeded in capturing Harpers Ferry and its twelve thousand defenders on September 15—the largest Confederate haul of Union prisoners in the war. But a copy of Lee's orders for this operation, apparently lost by a careless Confederate courier, had been found wrapped around three cigars by two Union soldiers in a field near Frederick, Maryland, on September 13. This extraordinary stroke of luck gave Union general George B. McClellan information on the separation of the Army of Northern Virginia into several parts. Although McClellan and his subordinates did not move quickly enough to save Harpers Ferry from capture, he did attack the badly outnumbered Confederates along a stream named Antietam near the village of Sharpsburg on September 17. In a battle with the most casualties on a single day in the entire war (approximately twenty-three thousand killed, wounded, and missing in both armies), the Confederates were forced to retreat on the night of September 18–19. Davis was disappointed by the failure of the invasion to achieve its grand objectives, but with the record of the summer's achievements in mind, he thanked Lee "and the brave men of your Army for the deeds which have covered our flag with imperishable fame."[13]

EVENTS IN TENNESSEE MAY HAVE ACCOUNTED FOR DAVIS'S decision to return to Richmond rather than continue on to Maryland to join Lee. As commander in chief, his place was in the capital rather than with a single army in the field. After Union general Henry W. Halleck's occupation of Corinth, Mississippi, at the end of May, Lincoln called Halleck to Washington in July to become general-in-chief of all Union armies. Ulysses S. Grant took command of Union troops in northern Mississippi, while Don Carlos Buell began a glacial advance toward Chattanooga to carry out Lincoln's cherished hope to "liberate" the Unionists of East Tennessee. Having taken command of the Confederate Army of Tennessee, Braxton Bragg began making plans to counter this effort. Confederate cavalry raids on Union supply lines by Brig. Gen. Nathan Bedford Forrest and Col. John Hunt Morgan slowed Buell's progress. These successes encouraged Bragg to devise a more ambitious goal than merely defending Chattanooga. He moved his army over a circuitous route to that city, leaving behind about twenty-two thousand men under Generals Earl Van Dorn and Sterling

Price to harass Grant and if possible to recapture Corinth. Once he reached Chattanooga, Bragg proposed to move north from there and "produce [a] rapid offensive . . . following the consternation now being produced by our cavalry." A Kentuckian, Morgan told Bragg that thousands in that state would join the Confederates as soon as a Southern army crossed the border.[14]

Davis was hearing the same information from his aide William Preston Johnston, also a Kentuckian and son of his late lamented friend Albert Sidney Johnston. Davis needed little persuasion. He too was convinced that Kentuckians under the iron heel of Lincoln's hirelings were eager to join the Confederacy. He had already reinforced the small army of Maj. Gen. Edmund Kirby Smith, commander of the Department of East Tennessee with headquarters at Knoxville.[15] Although Davis failed to create unity of command by placing Kirby Smith's and Bragg's armies under a single head (Bragg had seniority), he expected them to cooperate in a joint invasion of Kentucky. This cooperation, he told Kirby Smith, would "enable the two armies to crush Buells column and advance to the recovery of Tennessee and the occupation of Kentucky." To Bragg he added: "Buell being crushed, if your means will enable you to march rapidly on Nashville, Grant will be compelled to retire to the [Mississippi] river, abandoning Middle and [West] Tennessee. . . . You may have a complete conquest over the enemy, involving the liberation of Tennessee and Kentucky."[16]

This hopeful scenario seemed to be coming true in late August and early September. Kirby Smith's force captured Richmond, Kentucky, along with more than four thousand Northern soldiers on August 30. On September 3 they occupied the state capital at Frankfort and prepared to inaugurate a Confederate governor. When this news reached Robert E. Lee just days after his army entered Maryland, he issued a general order to his troops announcing "this great victory" that was "simultaneous with your own at Manassas. Soldiers, press onward! . . . Let the armies of the East and West vie with each other in discipline, bravery, and activity, and our brethren of our sister States [Maryland and Kentucky] will soon be released from tyranny, and our independence be established on a sure and abiding basis." Lee also issued a proclamation to the people of Maryland declaring that his army had come to help a state linked to the South "by the strongest social, political, and commercial ties" throw off "this foreign yoke" of Yankee occupation.[17]

Not to be outdone in the matter of proclamations, Davis issued his own to the people of Kentucky and Maryland explaining why Confederate armies had invaded their states. The South was "waging this war solely for self-defence," Davis declared, and "it has no design of conquest or any other purpose than to secure peace and the abandonment by the United States of its pretensions to govern [our] people." Confederate armies were in Kentucky and Maryland "to protect our own country by transferring the seat of war to that of an enemy who pursues us with a relentless . . . hostility." Davis appealed to the people of these states to "secure immunity from the desolating effects of warfare on the soil of the State by a separate treaty of peace" with the Confederacy.[18]

The responses of people in Maryland and Kentucky were

disappointing. Western Maryland was mostly Unionist in sentiment and few men from there joined the Army of Northern Virginia. Bragg wrote to Davis from Kentucky that "our prospects here . . . are not what I expected" from Colonel Morgan's promise of thousands of recruits. Bragg had brought along some fifteen thousand muskets to arm Kentuckians, but only fifteen hundred joined up. "Enthusiasm runs high, but exhausts itself in words," said Bragg in disgust.[19]

Bragg did achieve one success in Kentucky: the capture of the Union garrison of four thousand men at Munfordville on September 17. His continued advance northward threw a scare into Union forces at Louisville and created a panic in Cincinnati. But September 17 was also the day of the Battle of Antietam in Maryland, which forced Lee to retreat to Virginia. Three weeks later, Bragg's Army of Tennessee fought to a draw with Buell's Army of the Ohio at Perryville, Kentucky. Short of supplies, irked by the Kentuckians, and outnumbered by Buell, Bragg and Kirby Smith began the long retreat to Murfreesboro, Tennessee. Four days before the Battle of Perryville, a third leg of the Confederacy's offensive-defensive bid for victory had also collapsed when Van Dorn's and Price's effort to recapture Corinth had been bloodily repulsed.

Davis confessed himself "sadly disappointed" with the outcome of these campaigns. The chief administrative officer in the War Department said that the president "considers this the darkest and most dangerous period we have yet had." He was "very low down after the battle of Sharpsburg" (the Confederate name for Antietam). "He said our maximum strength

BRAGG AND KIRBY SMITH'S INVASION OF KENTUCKY, AUGUST–OCTOBER 1862

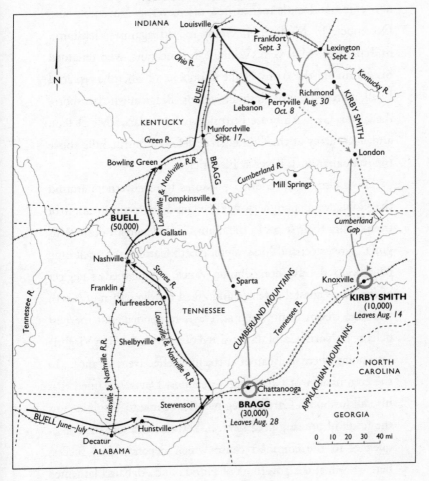

had been laid out, while the enemy was but beginning to put forth his."[20]

Confederate armies were forced to go over to the defensive again. The three main Union armies, two of them under new commanders, launched new offensives in November and December. In Mississippi, Grant moved against Vicksburg; in Tennessee, Maj. Gen. William S. Rosecrans, who renamed his command the Army of the Cumberland when he replaced Buell, marched out of Nashville against Bragg at Murfreesboro. And Maj. Gen. Ambrose Burnside, who replaced McClellan, aimed his army at the Confederate defenses on the hills above the Rappahannock River at Fredericksburg.

Davis also faced renewed pressures from governors around the Confederate periphery who resented the concentration of troops from their states in the main Confederate armies in Virginia, Tennessee, and Mississippi. North Carolinians, including newly elected Governor Zebulon Vance, complained of neglect of the state's coastal defenses and asked for the return of North Carolina troops from Virginia. Davis responded that the best defense of North Carolina consisted of a strong army in Virginia "at a point where they can offer the most effective resistance." To the commander of Charleston's defenses, Davis explained that his call for South Carolina regiments to come to Virginia "was the result of pressing necessity. . . . You can estimate the consequences to the common cause which depend upon success here."[21] When the governors of Florida and Alabama lamented "disaster after disaster" to scattered coastal areas that enabled the enemy to make numerous lodgments along their shores, Davis

commiserated with them but noted that "the enemy greatly out-
number us and have many advantages in moving their forces [by
water] so that we must often be compelled to hold positions and
fight battles with the chances against us. Our only alternatives
are to abandon important points or to use our limited resources
as effectively as the circumstances will permit."[22]

Davis's ambiguous explanation provided cold comfort to
these governors, who nevertheless remained loyal supporters of
the Confederate government. More troubling were the protests
and threats from Louisiana and Arkansas, largely cut off from
the rest of the Confederacy by Union control of most of the
Mississippi River. Nearly all Confederate troops still in Louisiana had been transferred to northern Mississippi after the fall
of Forts Henry and Donelson, enabling the enemy to occupy
New Orleans and most of southern Louisiana. The governor
bewailed "the calamity that has deprived us of our metropolis,
severed the State, and rendered all the banks of our navigable
rivers . . . vulnerable to the enemy's armed vessels." All thirty
Louisiana regiments were serving outside the state, he reminded
Davis, and "knowing the necessity of massing the Confederate
troops at vital points, I do not ask or expect soldiers to be withdrawn from our great armies" to defend what remained of Confederate Louisiana. But "no more men or arms should be spared
for distant service until the yet uninvaded part of the State is
guarded against marauders."[23]

The governor of Arkansas went even further and threatened
to secede from the Confederacy if the state was left undefended.
Most troops in Arkansas had been ordered east of the Mississippi

in April 1862 to help defend Corinth, and remained there even after that city fell. Union forces occupied northern Arkansas. The angry governor issued a proclamation deploring "Arkansas lost, abandoned, subjugated." She "is not Arkansas as she entered the confederate government. Nor will she remain Arkansas a confederate State desolated as a wilderness."[24]

Davis responded not by returning the troops but by sending Arkansan Thomas Hindman to command the Trans-Mississippi Department with his headquarters at Little Rock. A dynamo only five feet tall, Hindman declared martial law and ruthlessly enforced conscription. His methods aroused howls of protest, but he did create a new army in the state. The complaints caused Davis to send his old friend Theophilus Holmes, a North Carolinian who had proved ineffective as a division commander during the Seven Days' Battles, to replace Hindman.[25]

A genial but mediocre administrator, handicapped by near deafness, Holmes was soon whipsawed between the pressures of local defense and the demands for troops to help defend Vicksburg. In a command reshuffle to provide General Beauregard with a new position, Davis had promoted John C. Pemberton to lieutenant general and given him command at Vicksburg. Beauregard succeeded Pemberton in charge of the Charleston defenses. Pemberton had been unpopular in Charleston, in part because of his Pennsylvania birth. He had married a Virginian and had chosen to side with his wife's state instead of his own. This allegiance by choice rather than nativity was proof to Davis of the firmness of his convictions, but not to the prideful

Carolinians—nor to the Mississippians, who were suspicious of this "Yankee general" from the outset.

Pemberton faced a two-pronged Union campaign against Vicksburg in December 1862: Grant with forty thousand men was advancing overland from West Tennessee, while William T. Sherman with thirty thousand moved down the Mississippi River supported by a powerful naval squadron. Outnumbered two to one, Pemberton needed all the help he could get. Davis repeatedly urged Holmes to send him reinforcements—ten thousand men or more if he could spare them. But the president did not put this request in the form of an order, and was reduced to pleading with his Trans-Mississippi commander. The best defense of Arkansas, Davis told Holmes, was to maintain control of the Mississippi River between Vicksburg and Port Hudson, Louisiana. If Vicksburg was lost, the enemy "will be then free to concentrate his forces against your Dept., and 'though your valor may be relied upon to do all that human power can effect, it is not to be expected that you could make either long or successful resistance."[26]

Holmes resisted Davis's logic. He responded that he did not have the number of troops in Arkansas that Davis thought he had; many of those he did have were on the sick list; others were hundreds of miles away and could not get to Vicksburg in time; and—most important—they would desert if sent east of the Mississippi, and the people of Arkansas would revolt. The governor backed Holmes's arguments. "Soldiers do not enter the service to maintain the Southern Confederacy alone," he lectured Davis, "but also to protect their property and defend their homes and families."[27]

In the end the matter became moot. A raid by Van Dorn's cavalry on the Union supply depot at Holly Springs, Mississippi, forced Grant to turn back, and Pemberton's troops repulsed Sherman's attack at Chickasaw Bluffs on December 29. Davis acceded to Holmes's resistance to his entreaties. "If you are correct as to the consequences which would follow," the president acknowledged, "you have properly exercised the discretion which was intrusted to you."[28]

THIS AFFAIR BECAME INTERTWINED WITH ANOTHER DEVELopment that exposed flaws in Davis's leadership style. He buried himself in paperwork, spending long hours reviewing every kind of document that came into the War Department as well as his own office, sometimes as many as two hundred in a single day. Many of these papers concerned minutiae like the promotion of junior officers, bake ovens for soldiers in camp, details of army administration, and similar "little trash which ought to be dispatched by clerks in the adjutant general's office," according to the chief administrator of the War Department. One of those clerks noted that "the President sent a hundred papers to the department to-day, which he has been diligently poring over, as his pencil marks bear ample evidence. They were nearly all applications for office, and *this* business constitutes much of his labor. . . . He works incessantly, sick or well."[29]

As an administrator, Davis simply could not bring himself to delegate authority. His obsessive concern with military matters "induces his desire to mingle in them all and to control them," complained Secretary of the Navy Stephen Mallory. "This desire is augmented by the fear that details may be wrongly managed, without his constant supervision." This same absorption in details spilled over into meetings with his generals, which occasionally lasted late into the night. He met with individual cabinet members almost daily, and held two or three sessions weekly with the full cabinet. "These meetings occupied from two to five hours, far longer than was required," wrote Mallory. "From his uncontrollable tendency to digression,—to slide away from the chief points to episodical questions, the amount of business accomplished bore but little relation to the time consumed; and frequently a Cabinet meeting would exhaust four or five hours without determining anything, while the desk of every chief of a Department was covered with papers demanding his attention."[30]

Davis was far more preoccupied with army matters than with the navy; consequently, he granted much greater autonomy to Mallory than to the secretary of war. Mallory served during the entire conflict; five different men (not including one brief interim appointment) occupied the office of secretary of war. In effect, Davis was his own secretary of war much of the time. George Wythe Randolph became increasingly restive under these circumstances. In almost identical language, two War Department officials wrote that Davis reduced Randolph to the "humble capacity" of "a mere clerk." The president "issued

Stephen R. Mallory

orders, planning campaigns, as in East Tennessee, which he neither consulted the Secretary about nor apprised him of. He appointed general officers, sending their names to the A[djutant]
G[eneral]'s office without consultation, the first information the
Secretary received being that the commissions were brought to
him to sign."[31]

In September 1862, Randolph told a friend that he had
made up his mind to resign "because of the arrogance to which
he was constantly subjected by the President."[32] A dispute con-
cerning General Holmes's troops in Arkansas provided the occasion for his resignation in mid-November. Without consulting
the president, Randolph authorized Holmes to cross the Mississippi and join Pemberton for a campaign against Grant. This
plan was different from Davis's own efforts to persuade Holmes
to *send* part of his force to Pemberton but to remain personally
in Arkansas with the rest of them. Davis rebuked Randolph for
not checking with him before issuing the orders to Holmes.
Randolph immediately submitted his resignation. With an expression of irritation, Davis accepted it.[33]

"A profound sensation has been produced in the outside
world" by Randolph's resignation, wrote the diary-keeping War
Department clerk John B. Jones. "Most of the people and the
press seem inclined to denounce the President, for they know
not what."[34] Some editors and politicians who professed to resent
what they considered Davis's hauteur seized on the Randolph
case to condemn the president. Too busy—and disdainful—to
reply to his critics, Davis appointed another Virginian, James
Seddon, as secretary of war. The two men were acquaintances of

James Seddon

long standing. Although Seddon once complained that Davis was "the most difficult man to get along with he had ever seen," the secretary usually managed the relationship with tact and patience.[35] Seddon remained in his job for more than two years, the longest tenure of any of the five secretaries of war.

DAVIS CONFRONTED ADDITIONAL AWKWARD PERSONNEL issues in November 1862. Having recovered from his wounds, General Joseph E. Johnston reported himself fit for duty. But what duty? Johnston would have preferred reassignment to his old command, now the Army of Northern Virginia. But Robert E. Lee had made that army his own, and even Johnston recognized that reality. More problematic than what to do with Johnston were the loud rumblings of discontent with Braxton Bragg in the Army of Tennessee. Two of Bragg's principal subordinates—Generals Leonidas Polk and William Hardee—plus General Edmund Kirby Smith, whose Army of East Tennessee had operated jointly with Bragg's army in the invasion of Kentucky, blamed Bragg for the failure of that campaign. In truth, they were motivated in part by a desire to deflect well-deserved blame from themselves.

These early signs of dysfunctional command relations in the Army of Tennessee had deep roots. Part of the problem was Bragg's personality, which contemporaries described with a remarkable litany of adjectives: disputatious, cantankerous, irascible, austere, severe, stern, saturnine. But Davis had admired

Bragg ever since his volunteer Mississippi regiment had fought beside Bragg's artillery regulars at the Battle of Buena Vista in the Mexican War. Bragg's organizational and disciplinary skills had molded the best corps in the army that fought at Shiloh. When Davis decided to relieve Beauregard for taking an unauthorized leave after Shiloh, Bragg was a natural choice to replace him. Almost immediately, however, Beauregard's supporters in the press and Congress, who formed the beginnings of an anti-Davis faction, began beating the drums for Beauregard's reappointment—which required them to denigrate Bragg. "You have the misfortune of being regarded as my personal friend," Davis wrote to the general in August 1862, "and are pursued therefore with malignant censure, by men regardless of truth and whose want of principle to guide their conduct renders them incapable of conceiving that you are trusted because of your known fitness for command."[36]

Davis was therefore predisposed to take Bragg's side in the finger-pointing about who was responsible for the failure of the Kentucky campaign. But that position was complicated by his long-standing friendship with Polk, who was the main figure in the anti-Bragg cabal. The Kentucky lobby in Richmond, which included Davis's aide William Preston Johnston, also resented Bragg because of his outspoken criticism of the Kentuckians' reluctance to come to his support during the invasion. Davis summoned Bragg, Polk, and Kirby Smith separately to Richmond and tried to smooth over their conflicts. He acknowledged that "another Genl. might excite more enthusiasm, but as all have their defects I have not seen how to make a change with advantage." Beauregard would not do. He "was tried as commander of the Army of the West and left it without leave when the troops were demoralized and the country he was sent to protect was threatened with conquest."[37] Davis urged Polk and Kirby Smith to give Bragg their cordial support for the good of the cause, and rewarded (bribed?) them in advance with promotions to lieutenant general.

Recognizing that these moves might not accomplish the purpose, Davis attempted to resolve both of his personnel problems by appointing Johnston commander of the new Department of the West embracing all of the territory between the Mississippi River and the Appalachian Mountains. Johnston's mission would be to coordinate the actions of the three main Confederate armies in this vast region: Bragg's Army of Tennessee, Kirby Smith's Army of East Tennesee, and Pemberton's Army of Mississippi. Johnston thought that this command should also include Holmes's Trans-Mississippi Department so that Holmes could be ordered to cooperate with Pemberton in the defense of Vicksburg. Although Davis favored such cooperation, he decided—perhaps unwisely—to keep the Trans-Mississippi separate.

On paper, Johnston's new assignment appeared to be the largest and most important of the war. But he began to complain almost from the first that his real authority was minimal. Davis's requirement that all three army commanders should continue to report directly to Richmond as well as to Johnston seemed to lend substance to this complaint. Nevertheless, Johnston could have made more of this command if he had chosen resolutely to do so.[38]

To sort out some of these issues and to rally flagging Southern spirits, Davis decided to make a trip to Johnston's new theater, accompanied part of the time by the general. Leaving Richmond on December 9, Davis went first to Bragg's headquarters at Murfreesboro, Tennessee. He reviewed the army and found it in better condition and less threatened by the enemy than he expected. Indeed, Davis thought that Pemberton was more vulnerable than Bragg, and wanted to send a large division of nine thousand men from Murfreesboro to reinforce Pemberton. Both Bragg and Johnston protested that this detachment might fatally weaken Bragg and that Pemberton should be reinforced by troops from Holmes in Arkansas. Davis had of course already tried to get Holmes to send some of his men across the river, but without success. He overruled Johnston's objections and ordered the division to Vicksburg. Part of it arrived in time to help repel Sherman's attack at Chickasaw Bluffs on December 29. But Bragg would sorely miss the division in the Battle of Murfreesboro (called Stones River by the Federals) December 31–January 2, when its absence may have made the difference between victory and defeat.[39]

Davis's rejection of Johnston's advice in this matter of reinforcing Pemberton seemed to confirm the general's belief that his theater command was merely nominal. In any event, the two men went on to Mississippi to inspect Vicksburg's defenses. At several places during this trip and during his return journey to Richmond, where he arrived January 4, Davis gave speeches intended to lift morale and support for the war effort. One of the purposes of the trip, as he had explained to General Lee before he departed, was "to arouse all classes to united and desperate resistance."[40]

The best way to do this, Davis believed, was to recite a long list of Yankee atrocities. He had used this rhetorical device since almost the beginning of the war. As early as July 1861 he had informed the Confederate Congress that the Federals were acting "with a savage ferocity unknown to modern civilization . . . committing arson and rapine, the destruction of private houses and property. . . . Mankind will shudder to hear the tales of outrages committed on defenseless females by soldiers of the United States" and of whispered words in the ears of slaves "to incite a servile insurrection in our midst."[41] In the war's first year, however, Davis more often focused on themes of constitutional liberty, state sovereignty, and self-government as motives for fighting. But when his own government was compelled to enact conscription, suspend the writ of habeas corpus, and arrest opponents of the war, Davis came under attack for violating the very principles he professed to be fighting for. In consequence, his rhetoric shifted toward an emphasis on enemy atrocities as "a means to unite the southern people, strengthen their determination to resist, and prove the justice of the Confederate cause."[42]

This emphasis was much in evidence in Davis's speeches during the western trip. In response to an invitation from the Mississippi legislature, he spoke to an overflow crowd in Jackson the day after Christmas. "The dirty Yankee invaders" were a "traditionless and homeless race" descended from English Puritans "gathered together by Cromwell from the bogs and fens" of Britain, Davis declared. "They persecuted Catholics in England, and they hung Quakers and witches in America." Now they were waging a war "for conquest and your subjugation, with a malignant ferocity and with a disregard and a contempt for the usages of civilization." Davis was just getting warmed up. When he arrived back in Richmond, he told a crowd gathered to greet him that "you fight against the offscourings of the earth.—(Applause.) . . . By showing themselves so utterly disgraced that if the question was proposed to you whether you would combine with hyenas or Yankees, I trust every Virginian would say, give us the hyenas.—(Cries of 'Good! good!' and applause.)"[43]

While in Mississippi, Davis had taken time out from his consultations with Johnston and Pemberton to issue a proclamation branding Union general Benjamin Butler "an outlaw" and a "felon deserving capital punishment." Butler had commanded the Union troops occupying New Orleans and southern Louisiana. He executed a Southern civilian for tearing down the American flag from the U.S. Mint, plundered property, seized slaves, and even armed them "for servile war—a war in its nature far exceeding in horrors the most merciless atrocities of the savages." If captured, Butler should be "immediately executed by hanging" and all commissioned officers serving under him should be treated as "robbers and criminals, deserving death; and that they and each of them be, whenever captured, reserved for execution."[44]

By the time Davis returned to Richmond, Abraham Lincoln had issued the Emancipation Proclamation, which included a provision stating that freed slaves would be accepted into the armed services of the United States. In a message to his Congress, Davis denounced Lincoln's proclamation as "the most execrable measure recorded in the history of guilty man." It was the last straw among every conceivable atrocity committed by the armed forces of the United States. It was the "fullest vindication" of the South's decision to secede in 1861, because it provided "the complete and crowning proof of the true nature" of Northern designs to abolish slavery. Davis announced an intention to "deliver to the several State authorities all commissioned officers of the United States that may hereafter be captured by our forces in any of the States embraced by the proclamation" to be punished as "criminals engaged in exciting servile insurrection"—for which the punishment was death.[45]

Davis was particularly incensed by the Union plan to recruit former slaves as soldiers. When a raid by Confederate troops on Union-occupied St. Catherines Island off the coast of Georgia in November 1862 captured six black soldiers, the commanding general telegraphed Richmond for instructions on what to do with them. The new secretary of war, James Seddon, consulted Davis, who told him to make the following reply: "They cannot be recognized in any way as soldiers subject to the rules of war and to trial by military courts. . . . Summary execution must therefore be inflicted on those taken."[46]

Whether the six black men were actually executed is not

known. And whether the Confederacy would carry out such a draconian policy remained to be seen. Perhaps the war would soon be over and the question would remain moot. Confederate victories at the Battles of Fredericksburg and Chickasaw Bluffs, and the drawn Battle of Stones River (Murfreesboro), which Davis considered a victory, had produced demoralization in the North. The antiwar Copperhead movement mushroomed in strength, giving rise to hope in the South that the Lincoln administration would be forced to negotiate peace. Davis faced the new year with reviving confidence. "It is not possible," he told Mississippians at the end of 1862, "that a war of the dimensions that this one has assumed, of proportions so gigantic, can be very long protracted. The combatants must be soon exhausted. But it is impossible, with a cause like ours, we can be the first to cry, 'Hold, enough.'"[47]

4.

THE CLOUDS ARE
DARK OVER US

In Braxton Bragg's Army of Tennessee, the Battle of Murfreesboro produced bitter recriminations about missed opportunities that turned initial success into a retreat. After the Confederate attack on December 31 drove the enemy right back three miles, Union resistance stiffened and stopped the Southern onslaught. Bragg nevertheless telegraphed a report of victory to Richmond, where it caused "great exaltation." He added that the enemy "is falling back."[1] But the enemy was not. Rejecting the advice of subordinates, Bragg ordered another attack on January 2, which was shredded by Union artillery on high ground across the Stones River. With supplies running short and Union reinforcements arriving, Bragg decided to withdraw south thirty miles to a new base at Tullahoma.

Twice in three months the Army of Tennessee had apparently snatched defeat from the jaws of victory. And twice Bragg and his senior generals blamed one another. So divisive and open did the contention become that Davis ordered Joseph Johnston to visit the army, "decide what the best interests of the service require, and give me the advice which I need at this juncture."[2] The disaffected generals led by Davis's friend Leonidas Polk wanted Johnston to replace Bragg. Bragg himself hinted at a willingness to accept this solution.[3]

Davis had good reason to believe that Johnston would jump at the chance. He had continued to complain about his anomalous status as a theater commander with responsibility but no authority and to express a desire for a real army command. "I cannot help repining at this position," which was "little, if any, better than being laid on the shelf," he told Senator Louis T. Wigfall.[4] With no chance of obtaining what he really "repined" for, a return to the Army of Northern Virginia, Johnston nevertheless refused to consider taking command of Bragg's army. Instead, after inspecting the troops and talking with corps and division commanders, he reported to Davis that the army was in good shape and the disaffection was a tempest in a teapot that was subsiding. The army's operations under Bragg "evince great vigor & skill," Johnston assured Davis. "I can find no record of more effective fighting in modern battles than that of this army in december. . . . The interest of the service *requires* that General Bragg should not be removed," especially after "he has just earned if not won the gratitude of the country." Johnston refused to acknowledge that there might have been some reason why Bragg had not won that gratitude. In any event, Johnston insisted that he would be dishonored by accusations of conflict of interest if, after investigating the army's condition, he were then to take command of it.[5]

A stickler for the fine points of honor himself, Davis nevertheless could not see how Johnston would violate that code by replacing Bragg. After all, Johnston's original assignment as theater commander authorized him to take field command of any of the armies under his jurisdiction when the good of the service required it.[6] Davis soon realized that Johnston's report of reduced tensions within the army was inaccurate. The tempest did not subside. On March 9 the president had Secretary of War Seddon order Johnston to take over the army and send Bragg to Richmond for reassignment.[7] But Johnston managed once again to avoid obedience to his commander in chief's wishes. When he arrived at Tullahoma, Johnston learned that Bragg's wife was seriously ill, so he could not be sent away. Then Johnston himself fell ill. On April 10 he reported that he was "not now able to serve in the field."[8] For weal or woe, Bragg would remain in command of the Army of Tennessee. And Davis's main attention shifted to Virginia and Mississippi, where Union armies were once more on the move.

UNION MAJ. GEN. JOSEPH HOOKER LAUNCHED THE FOURTH "On to Richmond" campaign in April 1863. Outnumbering the Army of Northern Virginia by almost two to one (Longstreet was absent with two divisions on a separate campaign south of the James River), Hooker left part of his army at

Braxton Bragg

Fredericksburg and crossed the Rappahannock upriver with the rest to come in on Lee's rear. The Confederate commander daringly divided his army, sent Jackson on a long march to attack the Union flank, caved it in, and drove the befuddled Hooker back across the river by May 6.

Although ill and abed, Davis was elated by this victory in the Battle of Chancellorsville. He sent official congratulations to Lee "and the troops under your command for this addition to the unprecedented series of great victories which your army has achieved," although regretting "the good and the brave who are numbered among the killed and wounded." The most important of these was Stonewall Jackson, who died on May 10 of pneumonia that set in after he was wounded by friendly fire at Chancellorsville. Nevertheless, Lee's success caused Davis to hope that "we will destroy Hooker's army and then perform that same operation on the army sent to sustain him."[9]

But ominous news arrived from Mississippi. Grant had crossed the river below Vicksburg and was advancing on that citadel, which constituted one of the last links between the eastern and western parts of the Confederacy, the other being Port Hudson two hundred river miles downstream. "To hold the Mississippi is vital," Davis declared. Could Pemberton repeat his checkmate of the first Union attack in December? Davis initially hoped that cavalry raids on Grant's supply line would stop him, as they had on the previous occasion.[10] But Grant had cut loose from his communications and was living off the land this time. Concern mounted in Richmond as the news from Mississippi grew more grave in the second week of May.

With the front in Virginia apparently stabilized for the time being, several officials suggested sending detachments from Lee's army to the West. Longstreet proposed to take the two divisions that had been operating south of the James to reinforce Bragg in Middle Tennessee. They could then undertake an offensive against Rosecrans that, if successful, might force Grant to loosen his grip in Mississippi. Secretary of War Seddon wanted to send these two divisions directly to Mississippi—nearly a thousand miles away. Lee opposed this idea vigorously, noting that Hooker still outnumbered his and was being reinforced, so that to weaken the Army of Northern Virginia by Longstreet's continued absence "is hazardous, and it becomes a question between Virginia and Mississippi."[11]

Lee proposed instead to reincorporate Longstreet's divisions into the Army of Northern Virginia. With additional reinforcements he would then invade Pennsylvania, where he hoped to win another battle on the scale of Chancellorsville. A successful invasion might drain troops away from both Rosecrans and Grant. It would strengthen the antiwar Northern Copperheads, who might force the Lincoln administration into peace negotiations. Lee came personally to Richmond for meetings with Davis and his cabinet on May 15 and 16. The president had been ill for the past month with inflammation of the throat and a recurrence of severe neuralgia, which threatened the sight of his remaining good eye. For several weeks he had been too weak to come into the office, but he had continued to work from his sickbed in the executive mansion. He roused himself for these conferences, where he wavered between the options of reinforcing Pemberton or invading Pennsylvania. But in the long discussions of these alternatives, Lee carried the day with Davis and most of the cabinet. Postmaster General John Reagan held out for the option of sending Longstreet to Vicksburg. He was from Texas and feared that the loss of the Mississippi River would doom the Confederacy. Davis shared that concern, but so strong was his confidence in Lee that he approved the invasion of Pennsylvania and planned to reinforce Pemberton from other sources.[12]

This decision did not mean that Davis thought the Eastern theater was more important than Mississippi. Both were crucial; and because his home (partly destroyed by Union forces) was in Mississippi, he remained preoccupied with that theater. Ordnance Chief Josiah Gorgas wrote in his diary after a conversation with the president in March 1863 that he was "wholly devoted to the defense of the Mississippi, and thinks and talks of little else."[13] After the repulse of the Union navy's attack on the Charleston defenses on April 7, Davis ordered five thousand men from South Carolina to Mississippi. He scraped together a few thousand from elsewhere, and on May 9 he had Seddon order Johnston to Mississippi to take personal command of Confederate troops there. Johnston arrived at Jackson on May 13 to find that Grant's army was about to capture the state capital and was preparing to turn west toward Vicksburg itself. "I am too late," Johnston wired Richmond.[14]

This pessimism set the tone for Johnston's efforts—or lack thereof—during the next seven weeks. He ordered Pemberton to evacuate Vicksburg and combine his army with Johnston's small corps to form a mobile force to defeat Grant, after which they could reoccupy Vicksburg. Pemberton was reluctant to do so because Davis had telegraphed him a week earlier that "to hold both Vicksburg and Port Hudson is necessary to our connection with Trans-Mississippi." Many Southerners were already skeptical of Pemberton because he was a Yankee. He feared that if he obeyed Johnston's instructions to abandon Vicksburg, he would be accused of treason.[15]

In any event, Grant's victories over most of Pemberton's army at Champion's Hill on May 16 and Big Black River on May 17 made the question moot. Pemberton's remaining troops were driven back into the Vicksburg defenses, where they repulsed Union attacks on May 19 and 22. Grant settled in for a siege, while Davis continued to send dribs and drabs of reinforcements to Johnston and to urge him to break through Grant's tightening cordon. Persistent illness added to Davis's frustration, and stress in turn no doubt worsened his health. Almost daily he sent telegrams to Johnston imploring him to do something, messages to Bragg asking if he could spare reinforcements for Johnston, and missives to Governor John Pettus asking him to organize state militia to join Johnston.[16]

Little came of these efforts: Bragg could not send any more men without jeopardizing his own position at Tullahoma; Pettus had already scraped the bottom of the militia barrel; and from Johnston came very little information except that the 23,000 troops he had patched together were too few to attack the 30,000 under Sherman that Grant had put in place to protect the rear of his 40,000 besieging Pemberton's 30,000 at

THE VICKSBURG CAMPAIGN, APRIL–JULY 1863

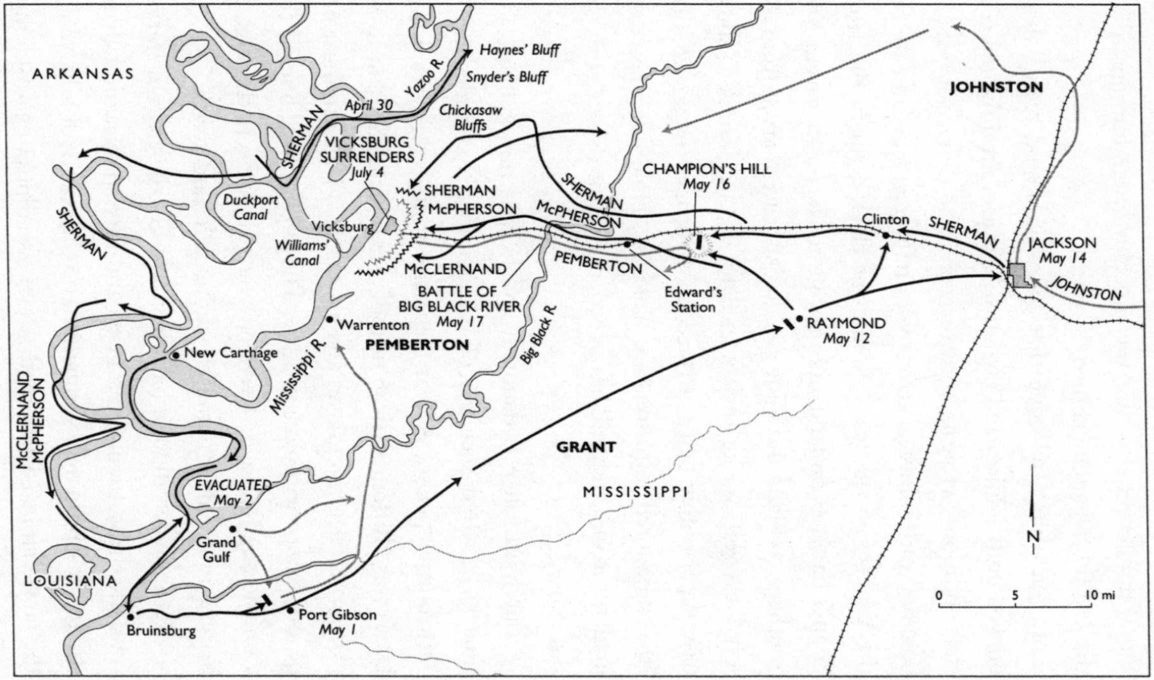

Vicksburg. Davis believed that Johnston had 31,000 men; the actual number of effectives was probably fewer, but more than the 23,000 Johnston claimed.[17]

In Vicksburg the hope that Johnston would rescue them buoyed both soldiers and civilians. "We are certainly in a critical condition," wrote an army surgeon in his diary, but "we can hold out until Johnston arrives with reinforcements and attacks the Yankees in the rear." Round-the-clock artillery fire from Grant's batteries on land and navy gunboats on the river drove Southern civilians and soldiers alike into caves carved from the soft loess soil, where they waited for rescue. The Vicksburg newspaper—now being printed on wallpaper—reported that "the undaunted Johnston is at hand. . . . Hold out a few days longer, and our lines will be opened, the enemy driven away, the siege raised."[18]

But Johnston was daunted, and he was not at hand. On June 15 he wired Secretary of War Seddon: "I consider saving Vicksburg hopeless." A War Department official reported that Davis was "furious with Johnston." He directed Seddon to reply: "Your telegram grieves and alarms us. Vicksburg must not be lost, at least without a struggle. The interest and honor of the Confederacy forbid it. I rely on you still to avert the loss. If better resource does not offer, you must hazard attack."[19]

But Johnston did not hazard attack. On the verge of starvation, the thirty thousand soldiers and three thousand civilians still in Vicksburg were surrendered on the Fourth of July. When the news reached Richmond, Davis was "bitter against Johnston," according to Ordnance Chief Josiah Gorgas. "When I said that Vicksburg fell apparently from want alone of provisions, he remarked 'Yes, from want of provisions inside and a general outside who wouldn't fight.'"[20]

Johnston retreated to Jackson; Sherman pursued and began to surround the city. Hoping to salvage something from "the disastrous termination of the siege of Vicksburg," Davis urged Johnston to hold the state capital if possible. "The importance of your position is apparent, and you will not fail to employ all available means to ensure success." But Johnston feared encirclement by Sherman's force, so he evacuated Jackson on July 16. He left so hastily that he failed to secure some four hundred railroad cars and locomotives, which the Confederacy would sorely miss.[21]

With the fall of Vicksburg, Port Hudson became untenable and surrendered on July 9. The Confederacy was cut in two: "The Father of Waters again goes unvexed to the sea" were Lincoln's felicitous words. Davis was profoundly depressed by these events. "Your letter found me in the depth of gloom in which the disasters on the Mississippi have shrouded our cause," he wrote to a friend in mid-July. "The clouds are truly dark over us." But they could not think of giving up. "Can any one not fit to be a slave, and ready to become one, think of passing under the yoke of such as the Yankees have shown themselves to be by their conduct in this war?" he remonstrated. The "sacrifices of our people have been very heavy of both blood and treasure . . . but the prize for which we strive, freedom and independence, is worth whatever it may cost."[22]

Davis relieved Johnston of his theater command, making

Bragg independent of him and leaving Johnston in control only of the troops he had evacuated from Jackson. Davis also wrote a fifteen-page letter in his own hand charging Johnston with what amounted to dereliction of duty in the Vicksburg campaign. Johnston replied, heatedly denying the charge. This exchange inaugurated what Johnston's biographer describes as "a paper war" between the partisans of the two men. Johnston's ally in Congress, Senator Louis T. Wigfall, called for publication of all the correspondence related to the campaign. Once an ally and confidant of Davis's, Wigfall had become one of his sharpest critics. He hoped to mine these documents for evidence to embarrass Davis and place the blame on Pemberton.[23]

Pemberton's hundred-page report, not surprisingly, blamed Johnston. Someone in the Davis administration leaked portions of it to the *Richmond Sentinel,* a pro-administration paper that made its position clear: "With an army larger than won the first battle of Manassas," Johnston "made not a motion, he struck not a blow, for the relief of Vicksburg. For nearly seven weeks he sat down in sound of the conflict, and he fired not a gun. . . . He has done no more than to sit by and see Vicksburg fall, and send us the news." Not to be outdone, someone on Johnston's staff apparently leaked a letter written by his medical officer that praised Johnston and excoriated Pemberton. This letter was published by several newspapers and inspired a vendetta against the general, who was all the more vulnerable because of his Pennsylvania birth.[24]

Davis regarded these attacks on Pemberton as an attack on himself. He continued to defend the general against the growing

J. C. Pemberton

opprobrium from all corners of the Confederacy. One newspaper quoted the president (perhaps not with literal accuracy) as stating, "My confidence in General Pemberton has not abated in the least—he is one of the most gallant and skillful generals in the service."[25] Public sentiment and army opinion turned against Davis on this issue, however. Two friendly Mississippi congressmen warned him that Pemberton "has entirely lost the confidence of the country." Davis failed to understand "the unhappy, disaffected, dangerous sentiment which pervades the whole people" on this matter. "You cannot uphold him. The attempt will only destroy you."[26]

Davis's opponents in Congress and the press did indeed use the Johnston-Pemberton controversy to undermine him. The vitriolic pen of John Moncure Daniel, editor of the *Richmond Examiner,* lashed out at Davis's "flagrant mismanagement." From "the frigid heights of an infallible egotism . . . wrapped in sublime self-complacency," Davis "has alienated the hearts of the people by his stubborn follies" and "his chronic hallucinations that he is a great military genius." Davis "prides himself on never changing his mind; and popular clamor against those who possess his favor only knits him more stubbornly to them. . . . Had the people dreamed that Mr. Davis would carry all his chronic antipathies, his bitter prejudices, his puerile partialities into the presidential chair, they would never have allowed him to fill it."[27]

The poison of this conflict seeped into the body politic of the Confederacy. Three months after the fall of Vicksburg, Mary Chesnut wrote in her diary that her husband, a member of

Davis's staff, told the president after an inspection trip "that every honest man he saw out west thought well of Joe Johnston. He knows that the president detests Joe Johnston for all the trouble he has given him. And General Joe returns the compliment with compound interest. His hatred of Jeff Davis amounts to a religion."[28]

IF DAVIS HAD NOT PREVIOUSLY GRASPED THE TRUISM THAT when things go wrong in wartime the chief blame will fall on the commander in chief, he certainly realized it now. He was also taking heat for the defeat at Gettysburg and for setbacks in Tennessee and Arkansas. Most disappointing was Lee's retreat from Pennsylvania after a failed campaign that left more than a third of his army killed, wounded, or captured.

Lee's invasion of Pennsylvania had started with great promise. With seventy-five thousand men he swept northward through the Shenandoah Valley, scattered the Union garrison at Winchester and captured almost four thousand of them, and moved into Pennsylvania during the third week of June. Confederate quartermasters gathered thousands of horses, cattle, and hogs and tons of other supplies from Pennsylvania farms. The army also captured scores of black people; claiming they were escaped slaves (many had actually been born in Pennsylvania), officers sent them back to Virginia and slavery. Initial reports of success that reached Richmond caused exultation. Even the *Examiner* praised "the present movement of General

Lee," which "will be of infinite value as disclosing the . . . easy susceptibility of the North to invasion. . . . Not even the Chinese are less prepared by previous habits of life and education for martial resistance than the Yankees. . . . We can carry our armies far into the enemy's country, exacting peace by blows leveled at his vitals."[29]

Lee thought so too. His reading of Northern newspapers had convinced him that "the rising peace party of the North," as he described the Copperheads, offered the Confederacy a "means of dividing and weakening our enemies." It was true, Lee acknowledged in a letter to Davis on June 10 as the army started north, that the Copperheads professed to favor reunion as the object of the peace negotiations they were urging, while the Confederate goal in any such parley would be independence. But it would do no harm, Lee advised Davis, to play along with such reunion sentiment to weaken Northern support for the war, which "after all is what we are interested in bringing about. When peace is proposed to us it will be time enough to discuss its terms, and it is not the part of prudence to spurn the proposition in advance, merely because those who made it believe, or affect to believe, that it will result in bringing us back to the Union."[30]

Lee concluded his letter with a broad hint that Davis "will best know how to give effect" to these views. Davis did indeed think he knew a way to offer the olive branch of a victorious peace at the same time that Lee's sword was striking Northern vitals. Not long after he received Lee's letter, Davis also read one from Vice President Alexander H. Stephens suggesting a mission

THE GETTYSBURG CAMPAIGN

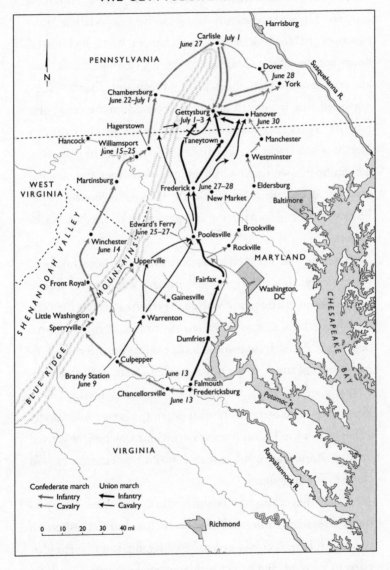

to Washington under a flag of truce to meet with his congressional colleague and friend from an earlier time, Abraham Lincoln. The ostensible purpose would be a negotiation to renew the cartel for prisoner-of-war exchanges, which had broken down because of the Confederate threat to execute the officers and reenslave the men of black Union regiments. But Stephens suggested that if Lincoln agreed to receive him, he could also propose "a general adjustment" to end the war on the basis of a Northern agreement to recognize the "Sovereignty of [a state] to determine its own destiny." Davis immediately summoned Stephens from Georgia to undertake the mission by joining Lee in Pennsylvania and looking for an opening to proceed to Washington.[31]

Stephens had not previously known about Lee's invasion. He protested that the Union government would never receive him while an enemy army was on Northern soil. On the contrary, said Davis; that was precisely the time to negotiate from a position of strength that would force concessions from the Lincoln administration. The cabinet backed Davis, so Stephens reluctantly agreed to go. It was too late to catch up with Lee in Pennsylvania, so Stephens headed down the James River under a flag of truce to Union lines at Fort Monroe, where he arrived on July 2 and had word sent to Lincoln requesting a pass to come to Washington.[32]

While this effort was being planned, Lee tried to pry as many troops out of the Carolinas as he could to strengthen his invasion force. Davis did order three brigades from North Carolina to join Lee. But he denied the general's request for a large number of Beauregard's troops from South Carolina, plus Beauregard himself, to come to Virginia as a diversionary threat to occupy Union forces that would otherwise confront Lee in Pennsylvania. Davis had already sent two of Beauregard's brigades to Johnston in Mississippi, and renewed Federal operations against Charleston made it impossible to strip its defenses any more. Lee also urged that some of the troops defending Richmond be added to his invasion force. But threatening movements against the capital by the small Union army on the peninsula forced Davis regretfully to refuse this request. "It has been an effort with me," the president told Lee, "to answer the clamor to have troops [already sent] stopped or recalled to protect the city."[33]

Whether any of these requested reinforcements would have enabled Lee to win the Battle of Gettysburg is impossible to say. After three days of repeated attacks that cost the Army of Northern Virginia at least twenty-four thousand casualties, the Confederates began their nightmare retreat from Gettysburg in a drenching rainstorm on July 4 at almost the same hour that Pemberton surrendered thirty thousand men to Grant at Vicksburg. Alexander Stephens's message asking for a pass to see Lincoln in Washington also arrived in the U.S. capital on July 4. Having just learned the news from Gettysburg, Lincoln replied curtly that Stephens's request was "inadmissible."[34]

The defeat at Gettysburg did not impair Davis's confidence in Lee—in sharp contrast with his loss of what little faith he had left in Johnston. In late July Davis wrote to Lee, "I have felt more than ever the want of your advice during the recent period

Gettysburg, Pennsylvania: Confederate dead gathered for burial at the edge of the Rose Woods, July 5, 1863

of disaster." Louis Wigfall reported that Davis was "almost frantic with rage if the slightest doubt was expressed as to [Lee's] capacity and conduct. . . . He was at the same time denouncing Johnston in the most violent . . . manner & attributing the fall of Vicksburg to him and him alone."[35]

Some newspapers, especially the *Charleston Mercury,* did express more than slight doubts about Lee's capacity and conduct in the Gettysburg campaign. Perhaps stung by this criticism, and experiencing health problems, Lee offered his resignation in a letter to Davis on August 8. "I cannot even accomplish what I myself desire," wrote the general. "How can I fulfill the expectations of others?" Without naming anyone, Lee stated that "a younger and abler man than myself can readily be attained" for the command. "My dear friend," Davis replied. "There has been nothing which I have found to require a greater effort of patience than to bear the criticisms of the ignorant," so he could empathize with Lee's feelings. But "to ask me to substitute you by someone in my judgment more fit to command, or one who would possess more of the confidence of the army, or of the reflecting men in the country is to demand an impossibility. . . . Our country could not bear to lose you."[36]

Yet another defeat on the Fourth of July added to the Southern cup of woe. Unaware of the surrender at Vicksburg, the Confederate commander in Arkansas, Theophilus Holmes, ordered an attack that day on the Union garrison at Helena as a diversion to aid Pemberton. The defenders easily repelled the assault, inflicting six times as many casualties on the attackers as they suffered themselves. This victory opened Arkansas to a Union offensive that captured Little Rock on September 10.

The situation in Arkansas had been a headache for Davis ever since he had promoted his West Point classmate Holmes to lieutenant general and appointed him commander of the Trans-Mississippi Department in 1862. Davis had a higher regard for Holmes's abilities than almost anyone else in the Confederacy—including Holmes himself. Complaints from Arkansas political leaders and Confederate Missourians about the general's incompetence scarcely dented Davis's confidence in him. One Missourian denounced the president as someone "who stubbornly refuses to hear or regard the universal voice of the people." Davis did go so far as to replace Holmes with Edmund Kirby Smith as commander of the Trans-Mississippi Department in February 1863. But he kept Holmes in place as head of the subdistrict of Arkansas. "I have an abiding faith that under the blessing of Providence, you will yet convince all fair minded men, as well of your zeal and ability, as of your integrity and patriotism," Davis told Holmes.[37] But Davis convinced no one, and he finally yielded to Kirby Smith's recommendation in March 1864 that Maj. Gen. Sterling Price replace Holmes.

After the fall of Vicksburg and Port Hudson, the Union navy patrolled the whole length of the Mississippi River. Gunboats effectively sealed off the two parts of the Confederacy from each other. Communications between Richmond and General Kirby Smith took weeks via a roundabout route by blockade runner through Galveston or even Matamoros, Mexico, or by smuggling across the Mississippi at night. Kirby Smith became the

Edmund Kirby Smith

head of a semi-independent fiefdom with quasi-dictatorial powers. He maintained good relations with the governors of Texas, Louisiana, and Arkansas (the latter two in temporary state capitals because Baton Rouge and Little Rock were occupied by the enemy). He established mines, factories, shipyards, and other facilities to supply and carry out military operations separate from those in the rest of the Confederacy, financed by cotton exports through Matamoros. "As far as the constitution permits," Davis told Kirby Smith, "full authority has been given to you to administer to the wants of Your Dept., civil as well as military."[38] In effect, Kirby Smith rather than Davis became commander in chief of the Trans-Mississippi theater. For the next two years "Kirby Smith's Confederacy" fought its own war pretty much independently of what was happening elsewhere.[39]

DESPITE ALL HIS OTHER PROBLEMS IN 1863, DAVIS'S BIGGEST command headache remained Braxton Bragg's Army of Tennessee. For almost five months after the Battle of Murfreesboro, this army and General William S. Rosecrans's Union Army of the Cumberland had licked their wounds and confronted each other twenty miles apart. Neither army undertook any major initiatives except cavalry raids on each other's communications. Bragg held a strong defensive position behind four gaps in the foothills of the Cumberland Mountains. In the last week of June 1863, Rosecrans, after much prodding by Lincoln, finally began an offensive. Feinting toward the western gaps, he moved

so swiftly through the others that the Confederates were flanked
or knocked aside almost before they knew what had hit them.
A Union brigade of mounted infantry armed with Spencer
repeating rifles penetrated deeply behind the Confederate position and threatened to cut Bragg's rail lifeline, forcing him to
retreat all the way to Chattanooga by July 3. In little more than
a week, the Confederacy lost control of Middle Tennessee—the
same week that climaxed with the Battle of Gettysburg and the
surrender of Vicksburg.

Bragg was unwell during this lightning campaign, and several of his principal subordinates performed poorly—especially
Leonidas Polk and William Hardee. The same two renewed the
backroom intrigues against Bragg that had long plagued this
dysfunctional army.[40] The infighting could not have come at a
worse time. The Confederate grip on Chattanooga appeared en-
dangered. The city had great strategic importance. It was located
at the junction of the Confederacy's two east-west railroads and
formed the gateway to the war industries of Georgia. Having
already split the Confederacy in two with the capture of Vicksburg, Northern armies could split it almost in three by a penetration into Georgia via Chattanooga. In mid-August Rosecrans
began a new advance with the intention of doing just that.

Davis was fully alive to the significance of this threat. He
instructed Johnston to send nine thousand troops to Bragg from
his idle army in Mississippi. On August 24 the president summoned Lee to Richmond for extended consultations. The front
in Virginia was quiet, and Davis asked Lee if he would be willing to go to Chattanooga and take command of the Army of

Tennessee. Lee demurred; Davis did not press the issue. Longstreet proposed that he take two divisions of his corps to reinforce Bragg. Lee initially opposed this plan as well. In a reprise of his argument before the invasion of Pennsylvania, he suggested that an offensive against the Federals in Virginia would relieve the pressure on Bragg. Davis leaned toward approval, but then changed his mind. Instead, he secured Lee's reluctant acceptance of the detachment of Longstreet. On September 7 Lee returned to his headquarters and set that process in motion.[41]

Events in Tennessee moved so quickly that it appeared Longstreet would not get there in time. Rosecrans feinted a crossing of the Tennessee River above Chattanooga but instead went across at several places below the city. As his troops moved through mountain passes toward the railroad that connected Chattanooga and Atlanta, Bragg evacuated Chattanooga on September 9. But then the Confederate general reached into his bag of tricks. He sent fake deserters into Union lines with planted stories of Confederate demoralization and headlong retreat. Rosecrans swallowed the bait. He sent each of his three corps through separate mountain gaps beyond supporting distance of one another to cut off the supposed retreat. Bragg intended to trap fragments of the enemy's separated forces and defeat them in detail. So corrosive were the relationships among Bragg and several of his corps and division commanders, however, that the effort broke down. Three times from September 10 to 13 Bragg ordered various subordinates to attack an isolated enemy corps or division; three times they found reasons to disobey Bragg's distrusted orders. Belatedly recognizing the danger, Rosecrans

THE TULLAHOMA AND CHICKAMAUGA CAMPAIGNS, JUNE–SEPTEMBER 1863

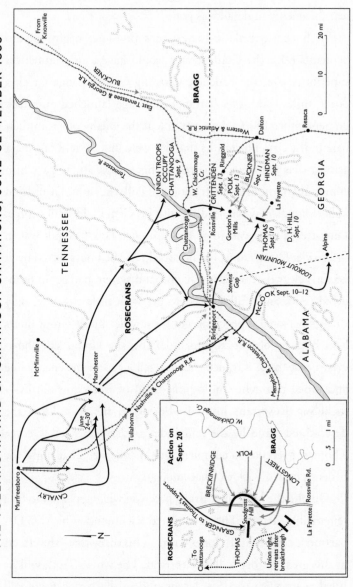

Action on Sept. 20

consolidated his army, and Bragg's "golden opportunity" to defeat the enemy in detail was gone.[42]

With the arrival of Longstreet's divisions beginning on September 18, the Confederates would have a rare numerical superiority over the Federals. Crossing Chickamauga Creek a dozen miles south of Chattanooga, Bragg launched an attack on September 19 in an attempt to cut the enemy off from their base in the city. The results that day were indecisive. Longstreet arrived that night with the rest of his troops. Bragg gave him command of the army's left wing and Polk the right. He ordered Polk to attack at dawn, leading with Lt. Gen. D. H. Hill's corps. Longstreet's wing was to go forward once Polk's assault was in full stride. Dawn came, but no attack. As the hours ticked by, it became clear that the army's command system had again foundered. Polk and Hill seemed to act with little urgency; only Bragg's personal supervision got the attack started—four hours late. Because of a mixup in orders on the Union side, however, Longstreet's advance encountered a gap in the enemy line and broke through, sending one-third of Rosecrans's army—including Rosecrans himself—fleeing to the rear. Only the determined stand by the remainder, under Maj. Gen. George Thomas, prevented a complete Union collapse. That night the Federals pulled back to Chattanooga.

Despite the bungling, Bragg had won what appeared to be a remarkable victory. The news elated Richmond. The War Department clerk John B. Jones wrote in his diary that "the effects of this great victory will be electrical. The whole South will be filled again with patriotic fervor, and in the North there will be a corresponding depression. . . . Surely the Government of the United States must now see the impossibility of subjugating the Southern people, spread over such a vast extent of territory."[43]

This optimism turned out to be wishful thinking. The Army of the Cumberland still held Chattanooga. The Battle of Chickamauga had cost the Confederates heavy casualties, so instead of renewing the attack Bragg settled down for a siege, hoping to starve the Yankees out. Instead of caving in, however, the United States government redoubled its efforts. Washington sent twenty thousand men from the Army of the Potomac to reinforce Rosecrans. It also sent Grant to Chattanooga. He replaced the discomfited Rosecrans with George Thomas, opened a new supply line, and summoned Sherman to Chattanooga with four more divisions. The Federals were clearly preparing a counteroffensive to reverse the results of Chickamauga and drive the Confederates deep into Georgia.

While these preparations went forward, renewed internecine warfare racked the Army of Tennessee's officer corps. Bragg demanded an explanation from Polk for the delay in his attack on September 20. Before replying, Polk met with Hill and Longstreet and concluded that Bragg should be removed from command. Polk wrote to Davis that Bragg must go. He even had the effrontery, in view of his own culpability, to claim that Bragg had the enemy "twice at his mercy, and has allowed it to escape both times."[44]

Meanwhile, Polk responded to Bragg's request for an explanation of his tardy attack by shifting the blame to D. H. Hill. Bragg considered this reply specious, and suspended Polk from command of his corps. He explained to Davis that although Polk was "gallant and patriotic," he was "luxurious in his habits, rises late, moves slowly, and always conceives his plans the best—He has proved an injury to us on every field where I have been associated with him." Davis telegraphed Bragg deprecating his action against Polk. The president was torn between his sympathy for Bragg and his long friendship with Polk, which caused Davis to estimate the latter's military acumen too highly. He resolved his conflicting feelings by telling Bragg that Polk should be restored to his post in order to avoid "a controversy which could not heal the injury sustained" and "would entail further evil. . . . The opposition to you both in the army and out of it has been a public calamity in so far as it impairs your capacity for usefulness."[45]

Before Bragg received this letter, ten generals and a colonel in the Army of Tennessee, including corps commanders Longstreet, Hill, and Simon B. Buckner, signed a petition to Davis calling for Bragg's removal. "Whatever may have been accomplished heretofore, it is certain that the fruits of the victory of Chickamauga have now exceeded our grasp," the petition stated. Bragg's personality "totally unfits him" for command. If he remained, the signers "can render you no assurance of the success which your Excellency may reasonably expect."[46]

Before he saw this petition, Davis had concluded that he must make the long trip to Tennessee to deal personally with the imbroglio. He stopped first in Atlanta to meet with Polk. The general asked for a court of inquiry, which he believed would exonerate him. Davis wanted no such exhibition of the

James Longstreet

army's dirty laundry. He decided to transfer Polk to Mississippi to serve with the remnant of Johnston's army. Davis then visited Bragg's headquarters at Marietta, Georgia. Bragg offered to resign—may even have urged Davis to accept his resignation to resolve the discord. But Davis rejected this idea. The logical replacement for Bragg would have been Beauregard or Johnston. Davis wanted no part of either. Instead, he hoped that he could persuade the malcontents to put aside their prejudices and act together for the good of the cause.

Davis held a meeting with Longstreet, Hill, Buckner, and Maj. Gen. Benjamin F. Cheatham (who had taken over Polk's corps). Bragg was also present. Contrary to Davis's hopes for harmony, the generals one after another (starting with Longstreet) expressed their lack of confidence in Bragg. Davis was startled, and Bragg must have been mortified. The president may have suspected that Longstreet was angling for the command, and was offended by his forwardness. In any event, despite this clear evidence of disaffection, Davis decided that "no change for the better could be made," and kept Bragg in command.[47]

Davis had brought John C. Pemberton with him from Richmond, apparently with the idea of giving him a corps under Bragg. But he changed his mind when he discovered that such an appointment would probably provoke a mutiny in the army. (Pemberton subsequently resigned his lieutenant generalship and loyally accepted an assignment as lieutenant colonel of artillery in the Richmond defenses.) Davis authorized Bragg to relieve Hill of corps command and to demote Buckner to division command. Bragg also reorganized other divisions and brigades in an effort to minimize dissension. Longstreet eventually took his two divisions on what turned out to be a failed campaign to drive the Federals out of Knoxville, which they had occupied since early September.[48]

With these departures and reorganizations, Davis and Bragg hoped for a de-escalation of the army's internal strife. The president urged Bragg to put the whole painful experience behind him and work with his subordinates toward a common goal despite lingering personal animosity. Davis's own military experience had convinced him, he told Bragg, that it was not "necessary that there should be kind personal relations between officers to secure their effective co-operation in all which is official." The recent crisis "should lift men above all personal considerations and devote them wholly to their country's cause."[49]

Davis continued his trip through the Deep South after leaving Bragg. He traveled to Alabama, Mississippi, back to Georgia, and then to South Carolina. He visited several towns and cities where he consulted with political leaders and military commanders, toured defenses, and gave public speeches praising troops from those areas, urging audiences to renew their efforts for victory, and predicting success for these efforts. He finally headed for home through North Carolina and arrived in Richmond on November 7, a month and a day after he had departed.[50]

Back in the capital the observant War Department clerk John Jones noted that Davis's decision to retain Bragg in command "in spite of the tremendous prejudice against him in and out of the army" was extremely unpopular. "Unless Gen. Bragg does something more for the cause before Congress meets a month hence, we shall have more clamor against the government than ever."[51]

Bad news followed Davis to Richmond. A Confederate attempt to capture the reopened Union supply line across the Tennessee River below Lookout Mountain was a fiasco. Grant continued to build up a powerful force in Chattanooga. On November 24 he struck. Northern troops under Joseph Hooker (who had come south with the reinforcements from the Army of the Potomac) drove the Confederates off Lookout Mountain. The next day George Thomas's soldiers in the Army of the Cumberland broke through the main Confederate line on Missionary Ridge with an attack that seemed to have no chance to succeed—until it did. The demoralized soldiers of the Army of Tennessee fled in panic, defying all of Bragg's efforts to stop them. Most of them did not stop until they reached Ringgold, Georgia, fifteen miles to the south.

The position where the breakthrough occurred was held mainly by Maj. Gen. John C. Breckinridge's corps. His dispositions were faulty and he appeared to have been drunk during the battle. Nevertheless, the chief blame came to rest as usual on Bragg's slumping shoulders. The general manfully accepted responsibility. "The disaster admits of no palliation," he told Davis, "and is justly disparaging to me as a commander." But the cabal against him must share the blame, he added. "I fear we both erred in the conclusion for me to retain command here after the clamor raised against me—The warfare has been carried on successfully, and the fruits are bitter." Bragg submitted his resignation; this time Davis promptly accepted it and appointed William Hardee as his successor.[52]

Public condemnation did not stop with Bragg; it went right up to the top. The fire-eating secessionist Edmund Ruffin declared that "the President is the first and main cause of this great disaster and panic, by his obstinately retaining Gen. Bragg in command." A North Carolina woman whose diary revealed close attention to wartime events had been a supporter of Davis until now. But "it is sad to myself to realize how my admiration has lessened for Mr. Davis," she wrote in December 1863, "since the loss of Vicksburg, a calamity brought on us by his obstinacy in retaining Pemberton in command, & now still further diminished by his indomitable pride of opinion in upholding Bragg."[53]

Davis had no time for regrets. He had to find a new commander for the Confederacy's second most important army, for Hardee had turned down the post because he did not feel up to the task of leading that troubled organization. The president again tried to persuade Lee to take the job. Lee responded that he would go "if ordered," but made clear his preference to remain where he was. He suggested Beauregard, but that officer remained in Davis's bad graces. The president asked Lee to come to Richmond "for full conference" on the problem. Lee assumed that Davis intended to order him to Georgia. If so, Lee talked him out of it. Instead, he urged Davis to appoint Joseph Johnston, even though Lee was fully aware of the president's distaste for the prospect. Similar pressures in support of Johnston came from Congress, from several high-ranking officers including Polk and Hardee, and from Secretary of War Seddon. Most other cabinet members shared Davis's distrust of Johnston's capacity. But the president finally recognized that he had no alternative. On December 16 he ordered Johnston to take command.[54] The die was cast; only time would tell if it would prove to be true metal.

5.

WE SHOULD TAKE
THE INITIATIVE

As commander in chief, Davis spent most of his time and energy on questions of strategy and command. But armies must be armed, fed, and supplied. Although he was reluctant to delegate authority on matters in which he took great interest, Davis did leave the main responsibility for logistics to his chief of ordnance, commissary general, and quartermaster general.

With the appointment of Josiah Gorgas as head of the Bureau of Ordnance, Davis made one of his best choices. Gorgas proved to be a master of organization and improvisation. He built an arms industry virtually from scratch and created an efficient fleet of blockade runners that by 1862 had ended the arms famine that initially crippled Confederate operations. Appeals went out to Southern churches and plantations to turn in their bells to be melted down and turned into cannon. Moonshiners responded to appeals to their patriotism and turned in their copper stills to make percussion caps for rifles. Southern women saved the contents of chamber pots to be leached for niter to produce gunpowder. The Ordnance Bureau located limestone caves in the southern Appalachians that contained niter deposits. Normally modest and self-effacing, Gorgas could not resist boasting of his achievements in the privacy of his diary. On the third anniversary of his appointment, April 8, 1864, he wrote that "from being one of the worst supplied of the Bureaus of the War Department," the Ordnance Bureau "is now the best. Large arsenals have been organized at Richmond, Fayetteville, Augusta, Charleston, Columbus, Macon, Atlanta and Selma. . . . A superb powder mill has been built at Augusta. . . . Where three years ago we were not making a gun, a pistol nor a sabre—a pound of powder—no shot nor shell (except at the Tredegar Works) we now make all these in quantities to meet the demands of our large armies."[1]

Gorgas's pride in what he had accomplished was fully justified. Although he was a native of Pennsylvania (who had married the daughter of a governor of Alabama), Gorgas faced none of the anti-Yankee prejudice that stung other Northern-born officers. But even his genius could not overcome the accelerating deterioration of Southern railroads and the consequent bottlenecks of transportation that created shortages of everything except ordnance for Southern soldiers and civilians alike. Before the war the South had imported nearly all of its railroad iron and locomotives from the North or abroad. Some of the Confederacy's prime iron-producing regions in Tennessee had been conquered and occupied by the enemy early in the war.

When rails, engines, and wheels wore out, replacements were not available. Blockade-running vessels, built for speed and stealth, could not bring in such heavy, bulky freight. Gorgas was able to keep Southern soldiers well armed through the end of the war because weapons and gunpowder had priority on what rail capacity there was.

More problematic were the commissary and quartermaster bureaus. Davis appointed his friend from West Point and regular-army days Lucius B. Northrop as commissary general. A man of congenial personality might have been able to overcome criticisms of the inevitable food-supply deficiencies in the Confederacy. But Northrop's personality was described as "peevish, obstinate, condescending, and difficult."[2] These qualities compounded the ill will directed toward Northrop by soldiers who held him responsible for their chronically short rations. "Northrop—what a bone of contention he is," wrote the diarist Mary Chesnut in 1863. "Even if the army is mistaken and Northrop is not inefficient—still if they believe it, something ought to be conceded to their prejudices."[3]

In truth, some of the problems with food supply were beyond Northrop's control. Thousands of square miles of grain- and meat-producing areas of the South were conquered and occupied by enemy forces. The fall of Vicksburg and Port Hudson cut off the main part of the Confederacy from western livestock. Union control of most of the Confederacy's navigable rivers and the blockade's interruption of coastal shipping forced transport of supplies onto the South's inadequate and worsening rail network.

Northrop did not help matters by establishing a centralized system of procurement and distribution. Warehouses were sometimes distant from the armies, especially the Army of Northern Virginia. The purchase of food closer to army operations where transport was less difficult would have been more expensive but perhaps more effective. When commissary agents *did* try to impress food supplies from local farmers or to seize them under the Confederate tax in kind, however, farmers sometimes hid their crops or livestock to avoid seizure. The rampant inflation that plagued the Confederate economy also made farmers reluctant to sell at government rates, which were invariably lower than market prices. In view of these structural problems, perhaps Davis was correct to defend Northrop and to keep him at his post despite widespread demands for his removal. But the president's stubborn support for Northrop seemed to be one more example of his favoritism toward incompetent friends.[4]

Ironically, Davis undercut one of Northrop's most ambitious efforts to feed the armies by trading Southern cotton for Northern food and salt. In October 1862 Northrop informed the president through Secretary of War Randolph that "the Army cannot be subsisted without permitting trade to some extent with Confederate Ports in the possession of the Enemy." Both Union and Confederate legislation forbade trade with the enemy. These laws were honored in the breach, however. And in any case, Randolph insisted, this prohibition did not apply to the government. "I think it will be found," he added, "that in European wars dealings between the Government of one nation and the subjects of another engaged in mutual hostilities are of ordinary occurrence." This "everyone else does it" argument did not impress Davis. Nor did Randolph's assertion that the only alternative to such a deal was "the Starvation of our armies." Before embarking on such a dishonorable course, Davis wrote, "the necessity must be absolute."[5]

Davis did approve a smaller arrangement by the governor of Mississippi to exchange cotton for Northern salt, but only because a French merchant acted as a go-between to provide the salt and export the cotton through a Confederate port. This fig leaf of legality satisfied Davis's sense of honor, but any proposition for direct trade "cannot be entertained." Northrop and Randolph's plan to trade cotton for commissary supplies fell through. "The President resisted it in toto," according to a War Department official. This refusal may have played some part in Randolph's decision to resign as secretary of war.[6]

Davis never did change his mind about the illegitimacy of trade with the enemy. But when General Edmund Kirby Smith's Trans-Mississippi Department became a quasi-independent fiefdom after the fall of Vicksburg and Port Hudson, Kirby Smith found that he could not feed armies or civilians without such trade. Some generals commanding local areas also approved various cotton-for-food trades on a small scale. Preoccupied with many different matters, Davis looked the other way.[7]

The shock of bread riots in the spring of 1863 was an eye-opener for the president. Drought in parts of the South the previous summer had curtailed food production. By the following spring, supplies were exhausted or priced at famine levels, and some people were literally starving. They suspected that storekeepers and government warehouses still had food that they were holding for higher prices or for the army. In a dozen or more places that spring, hungry women staged bread riots. Many of them were wives of soldiers. Armed with knives or revolvers, they stalked into shops owned by men they denounced as "speculators" and asked the price of bacon or cornmeal or salt. Upon hearing it, they denounced such "extortion" and took what they wanted.

Davis himself became involved with the largest riot, which took place in Richmond on April 2. On that morning several hundred women gathered in a church and proceeded to the governor's mansion to demand the release of emergency stocks of food from government warehouses. The governor said he could do nothing for them, whereupon the crowd's mood turned ugly. Shouting "Bread or blood!" and joined by boys and a few men, they smashed store windows and took shoes, clothing, even jewelry, as well as food. Hastily summoned militiamen appeared with their muskets. The mayor warned the crowd to desist or face the possibility of being shot.

At this moment Davis arrived on the scene. Although he was still recovering from a recent illness, he climbed onto a wagon and addressed the crowd. He promised the release of food supplies and appealed to their patriotism. He urged them to disband so that the muskets of the militia could be turned against the common enemy, the Yankees. A few small boys jeered him; the rest of the group maintained a sullen silence. Davis took out his watch and gave the crowd five minutes to disperse, or he would order the troops to fire. The captain told his men to load their weapons. Four minutes passed. Raising his watch, Davis said solemnly: "My friends, you have one minute more." Whether he would have ordered the militia to fire, and whether they would have obeyed—the crowd may have included some of their wives or daughters—will never be known. The assemblage melted away. Police arrested forty-four women and twenty-nine men as members or accessories of the mob; some of them may have served short jail sentences.[8]

The government released some of its stock of rice to civilians. Apprehensive merchants brought out reserve supplies of food, and prices dropped. The immediate crisis passed, but shortages and inflation continued to take a physical and psychological toll on the Southern people until the end of the war—and beyond. Two days after the Richmond riot, Congress passed a resolution calling on planters to convert part of their cotton and tobacco acreage to food crops. Davis endorsed this action and issued a proclamation appealing to farmers' "love of country" to carry the policy into effect. But neither Davis nor anyone else could resolve the intractable problems of transportation, distribution, inflation, and loss of territory that plagued the Confederate economy.

Meanwhile, the president faced a fight with Congress over a personnel issue in the War Department. The Confederacy's quartermaster general was Col. Abraham C. Myers, who had many of the same difficulties equipping the army with uniforms, shoes, horses, and wagons as Northrop did supplying it with food. Unlike Northrop, however, Myers was popular with Congress and unpopular with Davis. The reasons for the president's antipathy are unclear. Mrs. Myers and Mrs. Davis did not get along, and in the spring of 1862 Marion Myers was reported to have called Varina Davis "an old squaw." The president showed no immediate reaction to this rumor. In March 1863 Congress designated the rank of brigadier general for the position of quartermaster general, expecting that Davis would promote Myers. Instead, the president appointed Brig. Gen. Alexander R. Lawton to the post in August.

This action provoked a row with Congress. The Senate did not confirm Lawton, but Davis kept him in office anyway. Senator Louis Wigfall denounced the president's "petty tyranny & reckless disregard of law and contemptuous treatment of Congress." The Senate voted 15–9 that Myers was still quartermaster general. And seventy-six members of the House signed a letter to Davis insisting that he reinstate Myers. Davis refused, and in February 1864 the Senate finally confirmed Lawton— six months after he had begun doing the job of quartermaster general. Davis won this round, but at the cost of alienating many members of Congress.[9]

On another matter, however, Davis and his Congress were in harmony. On January 12, 1863, the president issued a proclamation stipulating that captured officers and men of black Union regiments would be turned over to states to be tried for inciting or participating in slave insurrections. Congress enacted legislation endorsing this policy but substituting military courts for state courts.[10] This change would have made no difference in the likely punishment—execution. But carrying out this policy proved to be impracticable. Union secretary of war Edwin M. Stanton ordered all exchanges of Confederate officers stopped so they could be held as hostages for retaliation if the Confederacy executed Northern officers.[11] The Davis administration decided to restore captured ex-slave soldiers to bondage instead of putting them to death—though in fact many were killed by enraged Southern soldiers rather than allowed to surrender. "Captured slaves should be returned to their masters" if they could be found, Davis informed one Confederate general. "Until such time, they might be usefully employed on public works."[12]

On July 30, 1863, Abraham Lincoln issued an "Order of Retaliation" stating that for every Union captive executed, a Confederate prisoner should be treated likewise; for every captive reenslaved, a Confederate prisoner would be placed at hard labor on public works.[13] This order was effective in preventing the *official* (but not unofficial) killing of black prisoners and their officers. But it did not completely stop reenslavement, because few Southern prisoners were remanded to hard labor in retaliation. The Confederates refused to exchange black soldiers under the exchange cartel negotiated in 1862. This refusal caused exchanges to cease, and the prisons of both sides began the descent toward overcrowding and tragic mortality that debased the last eighteen months of the war. Davis was unapologetic; sixteen years after the war's end, in his book *The Rise and Fall of the Confederate Government,* he continued to justify Confederate policy. "We asserted the slaves to be property," he wrote in

1881, "and that property recaptured from the enemy in war reverts to its owner, if he can be found, or it may be disposed of by its captor."[14]

FOLLOWING THE DEFEAT AT GETTYSBURG AND THE LOSS OF Vicksburg, morale plunged and cries for peace arose in parts of the Confederacy, especially North Carolina. The western part of that state, like East Tennessee and the portion of Virginia that became West Virginia, had contained many Unionists in 1861. And the rest of North Carolina perhaps included more reluctant rebels than any other Confederate state. The governor, Zebulon Vance, was a loyal Confederate who was nevertheless sensitive to the peace sentiment that proliferated in the latter half of 1863. Desertion from North Carolina regiments mushroomed. William W. Holden, editor of the state's largest newspaper, the (Raleigh) *North-Carolina Standard*, seized the leadership of a party that advocated peace negotiations with the United States. Holden vaguely claimed that such negotiations could achieve most of what the Confederacy was fighting for. But few except his true-believer followers shared that conviction. If the Confederate government failed to undertake negotiations, Holden declared, North Carolina should do so on its own.

In a letter to Vance on July 24, 1863, Davis condemned Holden's "treasonable . . . cooperation with the enemy" and asked the governor if such activities "render him liable to criminal prosecution." Vance replied with an admission that "there is a bad state of feeling here toward the Confederate Government." But "it would be impolitic in the very highest degree to interfere" with Holden or his newspaper, for any such repression would fan the flames of discontent.[15]

Davis accepted Vance's advice. But affairs in North Carolina seemed to go from bad to worse. Dozens of peace meetings took place around the state. A secret antiwar society named the Heroes of America flourished. Eight of the ten congressmen elected in 1863 from North Carolina were critics of the Davis administration; five of them were said to be in favor of peace. Vance decided that something must be done. "I will see the Conservative party blown into a thousand atoms and Holden and his understrappers in hell," he declared, "before I will consent to a course which I think would bring dishonor and ruin upon both state and Confederacy."[16]

But Vance could not act with a heavy hand, for he believed that a majority of North Carolinians supported Holden. At the end of 1863 he proposed to Davis a maneuver to outflank the editor. He urged the president to make "some effort at negotiation with the enemy" in order to allay "the sources of discontent in North Carolina." If the Lincoln administration rejected "fair terms" (which Vance did not define), "it will tend greatly to strengthen and intensify the war feeling, and will rally all classes to a more cordial support of the government."[17]

Davis missed the point of Vance's suggestion, perhaps intentionally. He was concerned with how such a gambit would play in the Confederacy as a whole and in the United States, not just in North Carolina. He had tried negotiations before, over Fort

Sumter in 1861 and with the aborted Alexander Stephens mission in 1863. Both were failures. To try again would be a confession of weakness, especially since anything resembling "fair terms" would be perceived as a Confederate retreat from its goal of independence. To send commissioners again "to propose peace, is to invite insult and contumely," said Davis, "and to subject ourselves to indignity without the slightest chance of being listened to." Referring to Lincoln's "Proclamation of Amnesty and Reconstruction" published on December 8, 1863, Davis asked: "Have we not just been apprised by that despot that we can only expect his gracious pardon by emancipating all our slaves, swearing allegiance and obedience to him and his proclamations, and becoming in point of fact the slaves of our own negroes?" No peace short of military victory was possible, the president insisted. "This struggle must continue until the enemy is beaten out of his vain confidence in our subjugation." Davis advised Vance to "abandon a policy of conciliation" toward Holden and his supporters "and set them at defiance."[18]

Davis followed his own advice. He asked Congress for authority again to suspend the writ of habeas corpus. Some judges—especially the chief justice of North Carolina—were issuing such writs to men who had received draft notices to enable them to avoid serving. The main purpose of suspension, however, would be to suppress the activities of "citizens of well-known disloyalty" who were seeking to "accomplish treason under the form of law" and "do not hesitate to avow their disloyalty and hostility to our cause, and their advocacy of peace on the terms of submission and the abolition of slavery." Congress quickly granted this authority for six months.[19]

Vance urged Davis "to be chary of exercising the powers" granted by the legislation. "Be content to try at least for a while, the moral effect of holding this power over the heads of discontented men before shocking all worshippers of the Common law by hauling free men into sheriffless dungeons for opinions sake." Davis considered this letter "discourteous." But he responded with assurances that he would use his power to suspend the writ sparingly, "with a due regard to the rights of the citizen as well as to the public safety." The president was as good as his word; few if any North Carolinians were thrown into dungeons.[20]

Holden suspended publication of his newspaper to avoid having the government shut it down. He also decided to run for governor against Vance. But the latter was a spellbinding orator who completely outclassed Holden on the stump. Vance managed to capture much of the peace vote on a war platform. "We all want peace," he told voters. The question was how to achieve it. Holden's plan for separate state negotiations would lead North Carolina back into the Union. "Instead of getting your sons back to the plow and fireside, they would be drafted . . . to fight alongside [Lincoln's] negro troops in exterminating the white men, women, and children of the South." The only way to obtain a real peace was "to fight it out *now*." Davis could only approve of Vance's offensive-defensive campaign. It did set Holden at defiance. In the August 1864 election, Vance swamped Holden at the polls.[21]

Davis also launched an offensive on another nonmilitary front far from North Carolina—in Canada. Perhaps infected by the virus of wishful thinking, many Confederate leaders were impressed by the apparent strength of the anti-Lincoln, antiwar Copperhead faction in the Northern Democratic Party. They proposed schemes to encourage this opposition by operating from across the border in Canada, hoping among other goals to defeat Lincoln's reelection in 1864. In February the Confederate Congress in secret session appropriated $5 million for operations in Canada. Davis approved the bill and appointed several agents, who made their way (sometimes by blockade runners) to the British provinces. Davis "was not sanguine of much success" in these enterprises, according to a colleague, but was "willing however to make the experiment."[22]

Davis's skepticism was justified. Confederate agents operating from Canada subsidized Democratic newspapers and peace candidates for office in midwestern states. They plotted the seizure of a Union gunboat on Lake Erie to liberate Confederate prisoners of war at Johnson's Island on the lake. They also infiltrated the crowds in Chicago during the Democratic convention in late August with the hope of liberating Confederate prisoners at Camp Douglas near that city. None of these schemes reached fruition. Confederate agents did manage to burn or damage a half dozen military steamboats at St. Louis, an army warehouse in Mattoon, Illinois, and several hotels in New York City. They also crossed the border from Quebec to rob the banks in St. Albans, Vermont. But none of these exploits advanced the

Confederate cause. Lincoln was reelected in 1864 despite all the efforts from Canada to prevent it.[23]

FOR DAVIS ALL SUCH ACTIVITIES WERE PINPRICKS AROUND the edges of Northern strength; the war could be won only by victory on the battlefield. Despite the low state of Southern spirits in the winter of 1863–64, he hoped that a counteroffensive in East Tennessee could recover the losses of 1863. As General William Hardee prepared to turn over command of the Army of Tennessee to Joseph Johnston, he reported to Richmond that the army had recovered both its morale and its physical readiness after the defeats at Chattanooga and Braxton Bragg's resignation a month earlier.[24] Almost as soon as Johnston arrived at Dalton, Georgia, to take command, he received a letter from Davis citing reports of the army's good condition, "which induces me to hope that you will soon be able to commence active operations against the enemy." The commander in chief reminded Johnston of "the importance of restoring the prestige of the Army" and, even more important, "the necessity for reoccupying the country, upon the supplies of which the proper subsistence of our armies materially depends."[25]

Johnston professed astonishment at the portrayals of the army's condition of readiness. To the contrary, he informed Davis, "it has not entirely recovered its confidence," the artillery "is deficient in discipline & instruction," the "horses are not in good condition," it had "neither subsistence nor field transportation enough" to take the offensive, and the enemy outnumbered him almost two to one. Johnston agreed about the importance of recovering East Tennessee. But he suggested that the best way to do it was an attack on enemy communications by General Leonidas Polk (now commanding the remnant of Johnston's previous force in Mississippi) and by cavalry leader Nathan Bedford Forrest advancing from northern Mississippi. As for himself, "I can see no other mode of taking the offensive here, than to beat the enemy when he advances, & then move forward." But "to make victory probable the army must be strengthened."[26]

When Davis read this letter he must have experienced a sense of déjà vu. He had heard many of the same complaints six months earlier to explain why Johnston could not move against Grant at Vicksburg. And the litany of deficiencies continued to flow from Dalton to Richmond for the next five weeks. The army did not have enough food and forage for men and beasts. Artillery horses "are so feeble that in the event of a battle we could not hope to maneuver our batteries. . . . More than half of the infantry are without bayonets." The army received only one-fourth the number of shoes each month needed to replace those that wore out. "The more I consider the subject the less it appears to me practicable to assume the offensive from this point," wrote Johnston on February 1. To get another perspective on the army's condition, Davis sent his aide Brig. Gen. William M. Browne to Dalton. His report painted a far more positive picture than that presented by Johnston. Browne agreed that the army was short of shoes, bayonets, and horses, but he found the men and animals in excellent shape and well supplied with food and forage.[27]

In the midst of this long-distance exchange about the condition of Johnston's army, Richmond received word from General Polk that Sherman had launched a raid with twenty-five thousand men from Vicksburg toward Meridian, Mississippi. Fearing that this raid was the beginning of a campaign to capture Mobile, Davis telegraphed Johnston asking (but not ordering) him to send reinforcements to Polk. Johnston demurred, claiming that he could not weaken his own force to help Polk. Davis replied sharply that the enemy in Johnston's front was inactive while Sherman's advance threatened Alabama. To stop him was "not only important in itself, but greatly conducive to your future success. If deprived of the supplies in the interior of Alabama and the Tombigby valley, the most disastrous consequences must ensue." Still Johnston hesitated, so on February 17 Davis peremptorily ordered him to send three divisions under Hardee to attack Sherman. Hardee's men got as far as Demopolis, where they learned that Sherman had returned to Vicksburg after destroying all railroad and manufacturing facilities in Meridian. Davis ordered Hardee to return to the Army of Tennessee. He remained angry at Johnston for the week's delay in sending reinforcements. If they had departed when Davis first urged Johnston to dispatch them, the president believed, they could have "met the enemy in advance of Meridian and Sherman's army would have been destroyed."[28]

During Hardee's futile advance to Demopolis, an important

addition to the army arrived at Dalton: Lt. Gen. John Bell Hood, who took command of a corps in the Army of Tennessee. As a brigade and division commander in the Army of Northern Virginia, Hood had been Lee's hardest-hitting combat leader. His arm was crippled by a shell burst at Gettysburg, but he had recovered in time to come to Georgia with Longstreet in September 1863. His division spearheaded the breakthrough that won the Battle of Chickamauga, but he lost a leg in the process. Undaunted, he spent the winter in Richmond recovering from his wound and learning to ride his horse strapped in the saddle with his prosthetic leg. The thirty-two-year-old general was befriended by the fifty-five-year-old president, who became something of a father figure to Hood. Davis's only form of exercise was riding, and on many afternoons he left the office for horseback excursions around Richmond. Hood began accompanying him on these rides, when the two would discuss military matters.

Impressed by the young general, Davis appointed him to corps command under Johnston. The president may also have invited Hood to keep him informed by writing letters without necessarily going through channels. Hood agreed to do so. After joining his corps, he also wrote directly to Secretary of War James Seddon and to Braxton Bragg, whom Davis had appointed as a sort of chief of staff in Richmond. To some commentators it has appeared that Davis commissioned Hood as a spy to send messages behind Johnston's back. But this kind of out-of-channels communication was common in the Confederacy, without nefarious purpose. Davis's previous experiences

J. B. Hood

with Johnston's lack of communication, and his distrust of the communications he did receive from the general, probably caused him to encourage Hood's missives.[29]

Soon after arriving at Dalton, Hood wrote to Davis that he found the army in "fine condition. It is well clothed, well fed, and the transportation is excellent." With reinforcements of ten or fifteen thousand men it could "defeat and destroy all the Federals on this side of the Ohio River. . . . I am eager . . . to take the initiative."[30] This was just what Davis wanted to hear. But where would reinforcements come from? Davis looked to Longstreet, whose troops were wintering near the Tennessee-Virginia border after failing to recapture Knoxville. The president wrote to Longstreet on March 7: "Our great effort should now be for a forward movement, as early as possible, into Middle Tennessee; and if circumstances permit it, into Kentucky." Davis outlined a detailed operational plan for the uniting of Longstreet's force with Johnston's for such an offensive. But whatever route the two generals chose, it was imperative that they should take "the initiative with the greatest promptitude and energy."[31]

Longstreet was agreeable. Indeed, he had proposed similar plans, including one scheme for mounting his entire command of fifteen thousand men on mules and horses for a raid deep into the enemy's rear. Not enough animals were available, however. In March Longstreet traveled to Richmond to meet with Davis, Lee, Bragg, and Seddon. All agreed that "we should take the initiative," Longstreet informed Johnston. But the latter believed that all of the plans for an offensive were "impracticable" because of inadequate logistics.[32] Hood was especially disappointed. "I have done all in my power to induce General Johnston to accept the proposition you made to move forward," he wrote to Bragg. "He will not consent. . . . I regret this exceedingly, as my heart was fixed upon our going to the front and regaining Tennessee and Kentucky."[33]

These words expressed Davis's sentiments as well. Meanwhile, he had to endure abuse from the press and public for his selection of Bragg as, in effect, a chief of staff. The *Richmond Examiner*'s sarcastic comment that this "judicious and opportune appointment" was "an illustration of that strong common sense which forms the basis of the President's character" was widely quoted. A North Carolina woman declared that "what we last week laughed at as idle & wild, a foolish rumor which no one heeded, is 'un fait accompli.' Gen. Bragg, Bragg the incapable, the Unfortunate, is Commander in Chief!"[34] The diary-keeping Mary Chesnut thought that Bragg would function as a "lightning rod: drawing off some of the hatred of Jeff Davis to himself." If that really was Davis's (perhaps subconscious) intention, it did not work. In any case, the appointment of Bragg made a certain amount of sense. He relieved Davis of some of the crushing paperwork; and whatever his failings in personal relationships with others, he got on well with Davis and offered sometimes astute military counsel.[35]

Despite disappointment with the failure to launch an offensive in Tennessee, Southern morale was buoyed by a victory over Union invaders of Florida at the Battle of Olustee in February, the recapture of Plymouth, North Carolina, in April, and the repulse of a major Union effort to capture Shreveport and penetrate into Texas in the Red River campaign in the spring of 1864. For Davis the satisfaction of these victories was marred by the personal tragedy of the death of his five-year-old son Joseph in a fall from the balcony of the executive mansion on April 30. The president had to surmount his sorrow and shoulder the heavy burden of running a war, for the military campaigns that could make or break the Confederacy were about to begin.

6.

WE MUST BEAT

SHERMAN

On May 4, 1864, the Army of the Potomac crossed the Rapidan River to begin a campaign against the Army of Northern Virginia that would prove unequaled in the war for its intensity and carnage. The next day the newly formed Union Army of the James moved up its namesake river toward the railroad lifeline between Petersburg and Richmond. These movements on the military chessboard posed an even greater threat to the Confederate capital than McClellan's Peninsula campaign of 1862 had done. Commander in Chief Jefferson Davis mobilized the Confederacy's dwindling resources to meet the threat. Excerpts from some of Davis's telegrams to General Robert E. Lee provide hints of his hands-on activities. May 5: "Two (2) brigades have been ordered up from Charleston." May 11: "Hoke's brigade left Petersburg this morning with other troops to effect if possible a junction with Ransom at Chester. . . . We have been sorely pressed by enemy on south side. . . . I go to look after defence. Will have supplies attended to at once and soon as possible send troops to you."[1]

On May 12 Maj. Gen. Philip Sheridan's Union cavalry was reported approaching Richmond from the north. Davis dashed home from his office and grabbed his pistols. He rode out to join the brigades of Generals Robert Rodes and Archibald Gracie. As matters turned out, they were able to stop Sheridan without the aid of Davis's revolvers. May 15: "Have directed all organized Infantry and Cavalry to come forward from the Department of South Carolina, Georgia, and part of Florida. . . . I am endeavoring to get out reserves in Virginia and No. Carolina, to guard lines of communication and depots so as to liberate veteran troops." These reserves were men and boys over or under conscription age and men with occupational exemptions from the draft.[2]

Davis brought General Pierre G. T. Beauregard from Charleston to command the troops he was assembling at Drewry's Bluff, seven miles south of Richmond, to confront Benjamin Butler's Army of the James. Davis rode out to these lines frequently to consult Beauregard and position troops; on one occasion he came under fire from Union artillery that took off the arm of a soldier standing near him.[3] Beauregard proposed one of his bold but unrealistic schemes to defeat Butler and Grant in turn. Lee would fall back from Spotsylvania toward Richmond and send ten thousand men to Beauregard, who would attack Butler. Once Butler was taken care of, Beauregard would join

Lee north of Richmond to destroy Grant. Davis vetoed the plan, which would have been likely to open Richmond's defenses to Grant long before Beauregard's shuttling of troops back and forth could have accomplished anything.[4]

Davis ordered Beauregard to attack Butler at Drewry's Bluff with the 18,000 troops he had, reinforced by 5,300 under Maj. Gen. William H. C. Whiting from Port Walthall on the railroad between Drewry's Bluff and Petersburg. Beauregard proposed instead to have Whiting assail Butler's rear while the main Confederate force attacked his front. Davis vetoed that plan too, because a Union force would be able to block Whiting's approach. He ordered Beauregard to bring Whiting to join his main force for the attack on May 16. Behind the president's back, however, Beauregard phrased his orders to Whiting according to his original idea. And just as Davis had warned, Whiting was not able to bring his troops to bear during the Battle of Drewry's Bluff on May 16. This battle was a Confederate victory, but less complete than it might have been had Beauregard not defied Davis's orders. Butler entrenched his army on a neck between the James and Appomattox Rivers, where they remained a serious threat to Petersburg.[5]

Nevertheless, the limited victory at Drewry's Bluff and Lee's staunch defense at Spotsylvania seemed to relieve the danger to Richmond, at least temporarily. Ordnance Chief Josiah Gorgas reported on May 20 that Davis "was in better spirits than I have seen him for a long time."[6] The Richmond front stabilized as the Army of the Potomac crossed the James River in mid-June to attack Petersburg. Beauregard's few troops managed to hold

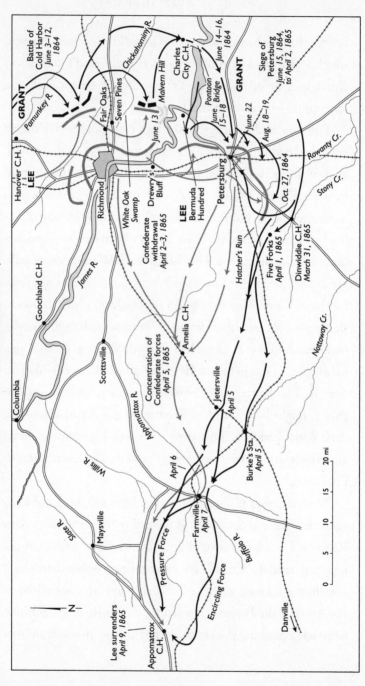

OPERATIONS NEAR RICHMOND, 1864–65

Battle of Cold Harbor June 3–12, 1864

Chickahominy R.

June 14–16, 1864

Charles City C.H.

Siege of Petersburg, June 15, 1864, to April 2, 1865

GRANT

Pamunkey R.

GRANT

Fair Oaks

Seven Pines

Malvern Hill

June 13

Pontoon Bridge

June 15–18

June 22

Aug. 18–19

LEE

Hanover C.H.

LEE

Rowanty Cr.

Richmond

White Oak Swamp

Drewry's Bluff

Bermuda Hundred

Petersburg

Oct. 27, 1864

Stony Cr.

Confederate withdrawal April 2–3, 1865

James R.

Goochland C.H.

Hatcher's Run

Five Forks April 1, 1865

Dinwiddie C.H. March 31, 1865

Scottsville

Concentration of Confederate forces April 5, 1865

Amelia C.H.

Nottoway Cr.

Columbia

Appomattox R.

Willis R.

Jetersville April 5

April 6

April 1

Burke's Sta. April 5

20 mi

State R.

Maysville

Farmville April 7

Buffalo R.

15

10

5

Pressure Force

Danville

0

—N→

Lee surrenders April 9, 1865

Appomattox C.H.

Encircling Force

them off until the Army of Northern Virginia filed into the formidable defensive works and forced Grant to settle down for a siege of Petersburg and Richmond that would turn out to last more than nine months.

During that time Davis often rode out to the lines at Richmond and occasionally came under enemy fire. Maj. Gen. Robert Ransom commanding part of the capital's defenses wrote that "there was no individual who was more familiar with the topography of Richmond and its vicinity than Mr. Davis. He had made himself acquainted with every road and by path and with the streams and farms for twenty miles around." Davis's private secretary Burton Harrison and members of his staff sometimes accompanied him on these rides to the front. Harrison described how the president "always led the staff as close to the ragged edge of danger as was humanly possible, having an apparent longing to escape from official thraldom and return to the risks of his days of soldiering."[7]

If Davis remained in thrall to paperwork, however, it still seemed to be more by choice than by necessity. The War Department clerk and diarist John B. Jones marveled at how "the President is indefatigable in his labors. Every day the papers he sends to the department bear evidence of his attention to the minutest subject, even to the small appointments." On another occasion Jones noted that "nine-tenths of the President's time and labor consist of discriminating between applicants for office and for promotion."[8] Little wonder that with only one functioning eye (and that one none too sound) Davis was plagued by frequent headaches and facial neuralgia. And the better spirits that Josiah Gorgas had observed on May 20 soon gave way to vexation with the news from Georgia.

As late as the first week of May 1864, Davis still hoped that General Johnston might be able to take the offensive against Sherman in northern Georgia. On May 4 General Leonidas Polk was ordered to bring his corps of fourteen thousand men from Alabama to reinforce Johnston, boosting the latter's strength to sixty-five thousand men to face Sherman's one hundred thousand. It was Sherman who took the initiative, however. He launched flanking movements that forced Johnston twenty miles south to Calhoun, Georgia, by May 16. Davis learned this news with "disappointment." He still hoped that "the future will prove the wisdom of [Johnston's] course, and that we shall hereafter reap advantages that will compensate for the great disappointment."[9]

Instead, the news grew worse. Johnston retreated another twenty miles to Cassville. There he turned to fight, assigning Hood the task of attacking the Union Twenty-Third Corps separated from the rest of Sherman's army. But Hood's scouts reported a Federal force on his flank, so he held back. This force turned out to be only a cavalry detachment, but by the time that information was sorted out, the chance for an attack had passed. Hood and Polk persuaded Johnston to pull back yet again to a more defensible position at Allatoona Pass through the mountains less than forty miles north of Atlanta. Johnston explained to Davis in a dispatch on May 21 that Hood "was deceived by a false report that a heavy column of the enemy had turned our right & was close upon him and took a defensive position. When the mistake was discovered it was too late to resume the movement." Johnston assured the president that "I have earnestly sought for an opportunity to strike the enemy" and would continue to do so.[10]

But Davis was getting contrary information from Hood. The general sent Col. Henry Brewster of his staff to Richmond to make a confidential report "in relation to our affairs."[11] Although no record exists of Brewster's report, its content can be deduced from the colonel's careless talk in Richmond parlors. Mary Chesnut reported that he said "Hood and Polk wanted to fight," but Johnston "resisted their counsel" because he was "afraid to risk a battle." These remarks were disingenuous, to say the least. But Davis was disposed to believe them. Johnston's alleged reluctance to risk battle seemed to be a reprise of his strategy in Virginia in 1862 and Mississippi in 1863. Secretary of War Seddon reinforced Davis's doubts. "Johnston's theory of war," said Seddon, "seemed to be never to fight unless strong enough certainly to overwhelm your enemy, and under all circumstances merely to continue to elude him."[12]

As Sherman advanced, his rail supply line stretching 60 miles to Chattanooga and another 150 miles back to Nashville became increasingly vulnerable. Earlier Confederate cavalry raids on such lines of communication had slowed or stopped Union advances. Johnston wanted to try it again—not with his own cavalry, but with Nathan Bedford Forrest's horsemen moving north from Mississippi. But when Polk brought fourteen thousand men to reinforce Johnston, he had left behind only about ten thousand, mostly cavalry including Forrest's troopers, to defend Mississippi. Union forces operating out of Memphis posed a serious threat, so Davis urged Johnston to use his own plentiful cavalry under Maj. Gen. Joseph Wheeler to raid Sherman's rear. Johnston maintained that most of Wheeler's cavalry were dismounted because of a shortage of horses, and he needed every mounted trooper for patrol and scouting duties. To a skeptical Davis, this seemed like one more excuse for doing nothing. Concerned about the defense of Mississippi, the president refused Johnston's request to turn Forrest loose in Tennessee.[13]

Insisting that stopping Sherman was more crucial than defending the marginal Mississippi theater, some contemporaries (and historians) were critical of Davis's failure to use Forrest against Sherman's communications.[14] One of those contemporaries was Governor Joseph Brown of Georgia, who lost few opportunities to throw darts at the president on issues ranging from the draft to the defense of Georgia. Maintaining that Atlanta was "almost as important" to the Confederacy "as the heart is to the human body," Brown accused Davis of favoring Mississippi over Georgia. Davis patiently replied, "I fully appreciate the importance of Atlanta. . . . I have sent all available reinforcements, detaching troops even from points that remain exposed to the enemy. . . . I do not see that I can change the disposition of our forces so as to help Gen'l Johnston more effectively than by the present arrangement."[15]

When Brown responded with a telegram lecturing Davis on his failure to understand that "Sherman's escape with his army would be impossible if ten thousand good cavalry under Forrest were thrown in his rear," Davis lost his temper. He telegraphed a withering reply to Brown bristling with the pent-up anger that he probably felt toward Johnston: "Your dicta cannot control the disposition of troops in different parts of the Confederate States. Most men in your position would not assume to decide on the value of the service to be rendered by troops in distant positions." Brown had the last word in this exchange. "I have not pretended to dictate," he wrote on July 7, "but when Georgia has forty to fifty regiments defending Richmond & Atlanta is in great danger probably no one but yourself would consider the anxiety of the efforts of her Governor . . . just cause of rebuke." If Davis refused to concentrate more troops to support Johnston, "I fear the result will be similar to those which followed the like policy of dividing our forces at Murfreesboro and Chattanooga."[16]

After stabilizing the front and holding Sherman in place at Kennesaw Mountain twenty miles north of Atlanta during a rainy June, Johnston pulled back twelve miles to the Chattahoochee River on July 4 in response to another flanking movement by Sherman. In reply to a telegram from Davis expressing alarm at this latest retreat, Johnston explained that Sherman's "greatly superior numbers" made it impossible to prevent such

THE ATLANTA CAMPAIGN, MAY–JULY 1864

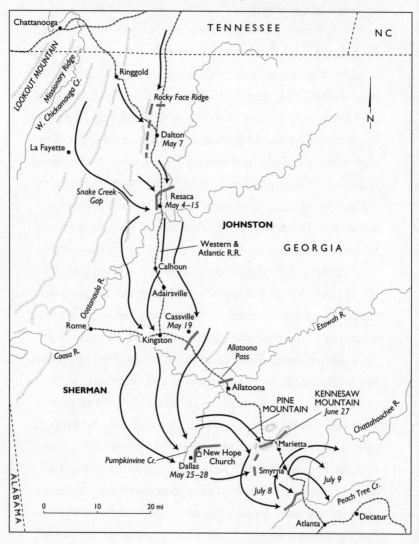

advances. "I have found no opportunity for battle except by attacking entrenchments," wrote Johnston, who again urged a raid by cavalry from Mississippi.[17]

For Davis this was the last straw. He sent Braxton Bragg to Georgia to survey the situation and advise him what to do. As Bragg headed south, Davis met the next day with a visitor who had just come north: Senator Benjamin H. Hill of Georgia. He had recently visited Johnston's army, where he discussed the condition of affairs with the general. Davis quizzed Hill, who was one of his strongest supporters in the Senate. Hill told the president that Johnston had assured him he could hold Sherman north of the Chattahoochee at least fifty-four days. With a wry face, Davis read Hill a telegram he had just received announcing that Sherman had crossed that river two days earlier and Johnston had completed his withdrawal that very morning.[18]

Even before he heard from Bragg, Davis decided that Johnston must go. But who would replace him? On July 12 Davis telegraphed Lee at his headquarters in Petersburg: "Gen'l Johnston has failed and there are strong indications that he will abandon Atlanta. . . . It seems necessary to relieve him at once, who should succeed him? What think you of Hood for the position?" Lee replied with regrets about the necessity and timing of replacing Johnston, and added: "Hood is a bold fighter. I am doubtful as to the other qualities necessary."[19] Lee followed this telegram with a letter elaborating his brief comments. "It is a grievous thing to change commander of an army" facing an imminent crisis, he wrote. "Still if necessary it ought to be done." As for Hood, he is "a good fighter very industrious on the battle field, careless off." Lee had had no opportunity to judge his capacity for command of an entire army, and suggested that "General Hardee has more experience in managing an army." Davis agreed that replacing Johnston "is a sad alternative, but the case is hopeless in present hands. The means are surely adequate, if properly employed."[20]

Bragg's reports confirmed Davis's convictions. "I cannot learn that [Johnston] has any more plan for the future than he has had in the past," Bragg wired the president. "The best interests of the country demand a change." In addition to holding long conversations with Johnston, Bragg spoke at length with Hood, who repeated his assertions that he had wanted to attack Sherman on several occasions but Johnston had held him back. Hood also said that General Hardee had agreed with Johnston. These self-serving claims were considerably less than the truth. Hood realized that Hardee was his chief rival for the command if Johnston was removed. And he probably knew that Bragg was receptive to criticisms of Hardee, who had been part of the anti-Bragg faction in the army the previous year. Bragg thus informed Davis that "Hood is the man. . . . I am decidedly opposed [to Hardee] as it would perpetuate the past & present policy, which he has advised & now sustains."[21]

Davis still hesitated. He knew that relieving Johnston would be controversial. It would intensify the hostility of the anti-administration coterie in Congress led by Senator Wigfall and now supported by a powerful trio of Georgians: Governor Brown, Robert Toombs, and even Vice President Alexander Stephens. Lee's caution about removing Johnston and his seeming preference, if removal proved absolutely necessary, for Hardee rather than Hood gave Davis pause. The president had offered the command to Hardee back in December. He had turned it down then and was a pro-Johnston man now, according to Bragg. Davis could have given the post to Beauregard, "but the President thinks as ill of him as of Johnston," commented the chief administrative officer in the War Department.[22]

Davis decided to give Johnston one last chance. On July 16 he telegraphed the general: "I wish to hear from you as to present situation & your plan of operations so specifically as will enable me to anticipate [events]." Johnston replied that "as the enemy has double our numbers, we must be on the defensive. My plan of operations must therefore depend upon that of the enemy. It is mainly to watch for an opportunity to fight to advantage. We are trying to put Atlanta in a condition to be held for a day or two by the Georgia militia, that army movements may be freer and wider."[23]

The Georgia militia? A day or two? To Davis this reply meant that Johnston was planning to yield Atlanta to the enemy. The consequences would be disastrous. The city was home to several war industries and was the nexus of a rail network radiating to every corner of the lower South. It had become a symbol of Confederate resistance second only to Richmond. Johnston's apparent unwillingness to defend the city or to strike Sherman a blow sealed his fate. With the unanimous support of the cabinet, Davis replaced Johnston with Hood.[24]

This act was perhaps Davis's most divisive and fateful proceeding as commander in chief. The press and public took sides and condemned or defended the decision. Congressmen and senators spoke out for and against it. Division also existed in the army, where Johnston was popular with the rank and file because, like Union general George B. McClellan, he was careful with their lives. But also like McClellan, he incurred the displeasure of his commander in chief because he would not fight. And whatever else Hood's appointment meant, it meant fight.

Two days after taking command, Hood attacked part of Sherman's army as it was crossing Peach Tree Creek just north of Atlanta. The assault was poorly coordinated and the Yankees repulsed it while inflicting almost twice as many casualties as they suffered themselves and driving the Confederates back into the Atlanta defenses. Another two days later Hood attacked again east of the city, bringing on the largest battle of the campaign. After initial confusion and retreat, the Federals steadied and counterattacked, again causing Confederate losses more than twice their own. Once more Hood attacked unsuccessfully, this time west of Atlanta on July 28, with the Confederates suffering seven times the number of Union casualties.

Davis had gotten more than he bargained for in the way of aggressive fighting by Hood. He wired the general on August 5 that "the loss consequent upon attacking [the enemy] in his entrenchments requires you to avoid that if practicable." Instead, Davis urged Hood to send his cavalry to raid Sherman's rail supply line, which would "compel the Enemy to attack you in position or to retreat."[25] Hood's horsemen under General Joseph Wheeler did raid Sherman's rear, but they did little to disrupt his supplies. Sherman's cavalry also conducted a failed raid south of Atlanta. And instead of assaulting the Confederate defenses, Sherman settled down for a siege. Atlanta remained in Confederate hands, which seemed to justify Davis's removal of Johnston.

In a masterpiece of understatement, Senator Herschel Johnson of Georgia, a Davis supporter, acknowledged that Hood's appointment did not "meet universal approval. It took the army & country by surprise, & produced momentary alarm." In the end, Johnson predicted, "nothing short of the success of Genl. Hood in closing the campaign, will procure a final verdict of approval."[26]

The apparent stalemate in front of Atlanta compounded the sense of futility and failure that spread through the North in the summer of 1864. Grant had bogged down before Petersburg and Richmond after the Army of the Potomac suffered sixty thousand casualties in two months with little to show for all the carnage. "Who shall revive the withered hopes that bloomed at the beginning of Grant's campaign?" asked a New York newspaper on July 12.[27]

Northern war weariness revived the prospects of Copperhead Democrats, who hoped to nominate a peace candidate for president and defeat Lincoln's reelection. A clamor for negotiations with the Confederacy became insistent. Lincoln had no faith in such a parley. He was running for reelection on a platform calling for "unconditional surrender" by the Confederacy and an amendment to the Constitution to abolish slavery in a restored Union. But the United States president could not ignore the pressure for peace. When Confederate agents in Canada convinced *New York Tribune* editor Horace Greeley that they were empowered to open negotiations, Greeley in turn pressed Lincoln to respond. He did so, specifying Union and emancipation as preconditions for any such negotiations. This proviso gave Confederates a propaganda victory by enabling them to accuse Lincoln of sabotaging the chance for peace by laying down conditions he knew were unacceptable to the Confederacy. So long as the war seemed to be going badly for the North—as it did in July and August 1864—this impression dimmed the prospects for Lincoln's reelection.[28]

Jefferson Davis had no more faith that negotiations could achieve peace with independence for the Confederacy than Lincoln believed they could achieve peace with reunion. But while Davis did not have to face a reelection campaign, he too was subject to pressure from Southerners who longed for peace. Vice President Alexander Stephens led an informal coalition that urged Davis to cultivate Northern Peace Democrats by agreeing to negotiations without insisting on Confederate independence as a precondition. Davis rejected this approach. Since independence would be an ultimate goal of negotiations, he maintained, it would be dishonest and useless to pretend otherwise.

Nevertheless, Davis did agree to receive under a flag of truce two unofficial envoys from the North whom Lincoln had allowed to pass through the lines. They met with Davis and Secretary of State Judah Benjamin in Richmond on July 17—the same day that Davis relieved Joseph Johnston of command. The Northerners began by asking Davis how peace might be attained. "In a very simple way," he replied in words recorded by one of the envoys, James R. Gilmore, a journalist who later published the interview in the *Atlantic Monthly*. "Withdraw your armies from our territory. . . . We are not waging an offensive war, except so far as it is offensive-defensive,—that is, so far as we are forced to invade you to prevent your invading us. Let us alone and peace will come at once." The envoys mentioned Lincoln's terms for peace: reunion, abolition, and amnesty. Davis's one good eye glared as he responded: "Amnesty, Sir, applies to criminals. We have committed no crime. . . . At your door lies all the misery and crime of this war. . . . We are fighting for INDEPENDENCE—and that, or extermination, we will have. . . . You may 'emancipate' every slave in the Confederacy, but *we will be free.* We will govern ourselves . . . if we have to see every Southern plantation sacked, and every Southern city in flames."[29]

The publicity generated by this meeting and by the Greeley encounter with Confederate agents in Canada made clear that no compromise peace was possible so long as Davis and Lincoln remained the heads of their respective governments. As Lincoln later put it in a message to his Congress, "the insurgent leader [Davis] does not attempt to deceive us. He affords us no excuse to deceive ourselves. He cannot voluntarily reaccept the Union; we cannot voluntarily yield it. Between him and us the issue is distinct, simple, and inflexible. It is an issue that can only be tried by war, and decided by victory."[30]

Except for the reference to himself as an insurgent, Davis

would have agreed with every word. And until September 2, the momentum of victory seemed to be with the Confederacy. Three days before that date the Northern Democratic convention in Chicago had adopted a platform declaring that "after four years of failure to restore the Union by the experiment of war . . . [we] demand that immediate efforts be made for a cessation of hostilities, with a view to an ultimate convention of the states, or other peaceable means, to the end that, at the earliest practicable moment, peace may be restored on the basis of the Federal Union."[31] This plank made peace a first priority and Union a distant second; "ultimate" and "the earliest practicable moment" might never come. A New York Republican denounced the tone of "surrender and abasement" in this resolution. "Jefferson Davis might have drawn it." Alexander Stephens proclaimed happily that "it presents . . . the first ray of real light I have seen since the war began." Even though the Democratic presidential nominee, George B. McClellan, reversed the priorities of peace and Union in his acceptance of the nomination, the *Charleston Mercury* declared that Democratic victory "must lead to peace and our independence" provided that "for the next two months we hold our own and prevent military success by our foes."[32]

But on September 3 a telegram arrived in Washington from General Sherman: "Atlanta is ours, and fairly won."[33] The previous day Union troops had occupied the city that had become such a potent symbol of Confederate resistance. Sherman had carried out one of his patented flanking movements, which cut the last open railroad into Atlanta at Jonesboro. To avoid encirclement of his army, Hood had evacuated the city on the night of September 1–2 after burning and blowing up everything of military value.

This single event had a huge impact on public opinion in both North and South. Combined with Admiral David G. Farragut's earlier capture of Mobile Bay and General Philip Sheridan's subsequent victories in the Shenandoah Valley, the capture of Atlanta reversed the midsummer decline of Northern morale and assured Lincoln's reelection. It had the opposite effect in the South. A Richmond newspaper lamented that "the disaster at Atlanta" came "in the very nick of time" to "save the party of Lincoln from irretrievable ruin. . . . [It] obscures the prospect of peace, late so bright. It will also diffuse gloom over the South."[34] Gloom was indeed plentiful. "Never until now did I feel hopeless," wrote a North Carolinian, "but since God seems to have forsaken us I despair." Mary Chesnut also despaired. "We are going to be wiped off the earth," she wrote. "Since Atlanta I have felt as if all were dead within me, forever."[35]

Many Southerners were sure that they knew whom to blame. Davis's removal of Johnston was the direct cause of the disaster, according to the *Richmond Examiner.* "Is it not cruelly hard, that the struggle of eight millions, who sacrifice their lives . . . should come to naught—should end in the ruin of us all— in order that the predilections and antipathies, the pitiful personal feelings, of a single man may be indulged?"[36] Davis was unapologetic about his decision to replace Johnston, who he believed had been preparing to abandon Atlanta. "I resolved that it should not" be abandoned without a fight, he said in a public speech. "I put a man in command who I knew would strike a manly blow for the city, and many a Yankee's blood was made to nourish the soil before the prize was won."[37] Left unremarked was the much larger amount of Southern blood in the soil.

Davis was more concerned about declining public and army morale than he was about his own growing unpopularity. On September 20 he once again left Richmond for a wearying trip on rickety railroads to the Deep South. His purpose was threefold: to rouse public spirits; to deal with command problems in Hood's army; and to settle on a strategy to counter the consequences of Sherman's capture of Atlanta.

The president gave more than a dozen speeches during this trip, from Danville, Virginia, to Montgomery, Alabama, and back through the Carolinas. They amounted to pep talks lauding the contributions of each community to the war effort, chastising laggards and croakers, urging absentees to return to the ranks, prodding able-bodied men not performing essential home-front duties to enlist, predicting the revival of Confederate fortunes that would drive Sherman out of Georgia and take Confederate armies to the Ohio River, damning Northern atrocities, and extolling the willingness of the Southern people to make sacrifices for the cause of liberty. Many commentators praised Davis's speeches and credited them with stirring up public enthusiasm.

At Macon, Georgia, Davis declared that if half of the men AWOL from the Army of Tennessee returned, Sherman would be destroyed. The Yankee general "cannot keep up his long line of communications, and retreat sooner or later, he must. And when that day comes, the fate that befell the army of the French Empire in its retreat from Moscow will be reenacted. Our cavalry and our people will harass and destroy his army as did the Cossacks that of Napoleon." Like the French emperor, Sherman "will escape with only a body guard."[38]

When General Grant read a newspaper report of this speech, he riposted: "Who is to furnish the snow for this Moscow retreat?"[39] Some Southerners criticized Davis for getting carried away in the Macon address. But he ignored the criticism and kept to the theme in subsequent speeches. The president worked it into his argument that peace with independence could not be accomplished by negotiations but only by military victories that would force the enemy to sue for peace on Southern terms. "Does any one believe that Yankees are to be conciliated by terms of concession?" he asked a large crowd in Columbia, the capital of South Carolina. "Does any one imagine that we can conquer the Yankees by retreating before them, or do you not all know that the only way to make spaniels civil is to whip them?"[40]

Some Southerners—particularly Alexander Stephens and Governor Joseph Brown of Georgia—continued to put their faith in the Northern Copperheads. Davis was skeptical, but he told an audience in Augusta: "Let fresh victories crown our arms, and the peace party, if there be such at the North, can elect its candidate. . . . We must beat Sherman, we must march into Tennessee—there we will draw from twenty thousand to thirty thousand to our standard; and so strengthened, we must push the enemy back to the banks of the Ohio, and thus give the peace party of the North an accretion no puny editorial can give."[41] In Greensboro, North Carolina, where peace sentiment was strong, Davis likewise predicted that Sherman would soon be "driven out of Tennessee and Kentucky, even across the beautiful Ohio, by our advancing and conquering armies. Then we shall have thousands of recruits . . . that will so augment our armies that our foes will sue for peace."[42]

It is not clear whether Davis believed his own rhetoric. But it did elicit cheers from the crowds. In his strategy meetings with Hood and other generals, however, the mood was more sober. One of Davis's purposes in making this trip was to sort out command problems in the Army of Tennessee. Back in July, General Hardee had resented the promotion of Hood over his head— even though the president had offered Hardee the position seven months earlier and he had turned it down. When Hardee had requested a transfer after Hood's promotion, Davis had appealed to his patriotism and professionalism in a successful effort to persuade him to stay.

But by September, matters had deteriorated further. Hardee commanded the corps that Sherman had beaten at Jonesboro to force the evacuation of Atlanta. Hood blamed Hardee for poor generalship, and Hardee in turn blamed Hood. After meeting with Hood at his headquarters in Palmetto, Georgia, Davis resolved the issue with a wholesale reshuffling of command

William J. Hardee

personnel. He left Hood in charge of the Army of Tennessee and transferred Hardee to a new post as commander of the defenses of Charleston and Savannah. Davis had recently brought Lt. Gen. Richard Taylor from the Trans-Mississippi (where he had been feuding with General Edmund Kirby Smith) to command the troops in Alabama and Mississippi. To take charge of the whole theater in which all these armies were to operate, Davis named none other than Beauregard, who had come south with the president after an uneasy reconciliation between the two proud men. It remained to be seen whether Beauregard would be able to make more of this "Military Division of the West" than Joseph Johnston had done two years earlier, when its resources and manpower were greater and the enemy occupied much less of it.[43]

Hood's army was the largest in this theater, and the third purpose of Davis's trip was to consult with that general about what to do with it. The president's public speeches, of course, predicted that it would invade Tennessee and Kentucky. Hood, and Davis himself, may have harbored a desire to do just that. But as a practical matter, there was the small problem of what to do about Sherman's army occupying Atlanta and pointing like an arrow at the heartland of the Deep South. Davis approved Hood's proposal to move north of Atlanta along Sherman's rail supply line from Chattanooga, destroying tracks and bridges and gobbling up the small garrisons along the way. This action, they believed, would pry Sherman out of Atlanta and force him to come after Hood. If Sherman decided instead to move south, Hood would follow on his tail and do all the damage he could.[44]

Hood started north on October 1. Leaving one corps to garrison Atlanta, Sherman followed. For the next two weeks the two armies skirmished and maneuvered back over the same territory they had fought over from May to August. Forrest's and Wheeler's cavalry also raided Union-occupied territory from northeast Alabama to western Tennessee. Sherman finally drove Hood off his supply line. But the Union general expressed frustration with this kind of warfare, which seemed to play into Confederate hands. "The whole effect of my campaign will be lost" if he continued to play that game, Sherman complained to Grant. "It will be a physical impossibility to protect the [rail] roads, now that Hood, Forrest, and Wheeler, and the whole batch of devils, are turned loose without home or habitation. By attempting to hold the roads we will lose a thousand men monthly and will gain no result."[45] Sherman pleaded with Grant to turn him loose to march through Georgia to Savannah, destroying war resources as he went. To deal with the possibility that Hood might ignore him and head into Tennessee, Sherman sent two corps under George Thomas to bolster Union defenses in that state.

While Sherman was persuading Grant and Lincoln to approve his march, the Northern presidential election took place. As Davis had expected, Lincoln won a decisive victory. The Confederate president had perhaps even hoped for this outcome to dispel all notions of a negotiated peace and to harden

Southern resolve to fight on. In a message to his Congress, Davis declared that the Confederacy remained "as erect and defiant as ever. Nothing [has] changed in the purpose of its Government, in the indomitable valor of its troops, or in the unquenchable spirit of its people. . . . There is no military success of the enemy which can accomplish its destruction."[46]

It was this last-ditch defiance that Sherman set out to break in his march from Atlanta to the sea.

7.

THE LAST RESORT

As Sherman departed Atlanta southward in the third week of November, Hood turned his back and began to move north into Tennessee. This action was contrary to the strategy agreed upon by Davis and Hood in their meeting at Hood's headquarters on September 25, which required Hood to follow on Sherman's heels if the Yankees moved south. But Davis's public speeches during his trip to the Deep South had alluded to an invasion that would take Hood's army all the way to the Ohio River. And in a letter to Hood on November 7, Davis seemed to endorse the general's intention to do just that. An invasion of Tennessee was consistent with the president's continued commitment to an offensive-defensive strategy, even though the Confederacy's waning resources made such a strategy totally unrealistic.[1]

Hood's campaign in Tennessee ended disastrously. In the

Battle of Franklin on November 30, his army lost twelve generals killed and wounded; at the Battle of Nashville on December
15–16, the Army of Tennessee was virtually destroyed as a fighting force. Hood retreated to Mississippi with fewer than half of
the forty thousand troops with whom he had started the invasion. On January 13, 1865, he resigned his command. In his
memoirs, Davis claimed that he had not approved of Hood's
campaign. But contemporary evidence contradicts this effort to
deny responsibility.[2]

Hood had left behind only Joseph Wheeler's cavalry and
Georgia militia to impede Sherman's progress from Atlanta 285
miles to Savannah. From Richmond Davis sent a flurry of telegrams to Beauregard, to Howell Cobb (commander of the militia), and to William Hardee (commander at Savannah) trying
to coordinate these efforts. He ordered the mining of roads
with "subterranean torpedoes" and the destruction of bridges,
livestock, and food crops in Sherman's path. These actions did
little to slow Sherman and much to anger him. Denouncing the
use of mines as "barbarism," Sherman forced prisoners to pre-
cede his soldiers to pry them up and defuse them. A Georgia
citizen informed Davis that Wheeler's horsemen had obeyed
Davis's instructions too literally. They burned "all the corn &
fodder, [drove] off all the stock of farmers for ten miles on each
side of the Rail Road," and took most of the horses and mules.
These exploits created such a backlash among the people that
they "will not care one cent which army are victorious." Davis,
however, believed that his orders had not been carried out thor-
oughly enough. If they had been, he maintained after Sherman

HOOD INVADES TENNESSEE WHILE SHERMAN MARCHES TO THE SEA, NOVEMBER–DECEMBER 1864

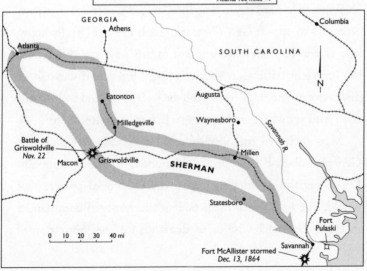

reached the sea and captured Savannah on December 21, "the faithful execution of those orders would have defeated his project."[3]

The failure of Hood's campaign and the fall of Savannah brought down a new torrent of censure on Davis's head. The replacement of Johnston with Hood was the cause of the disaster, claimed the *Richmond Examiner*. In fact, declared the editor, "every misfortune of the country is palpably and confessedly due to the interference of Mr. Davis." Several members of Congress echoed Senator Louis Wigfall's denunciation of Davis as "an amalgam of malice and mediocrity."[4] One of Davis's supporters lamented that the president "is in a sea of trouble. . . . It is the old story of the sick lion who even the jackass can kick without fear." Ordnance Chief Josiah Gorgas, although a friend and confidant of Davis's, deplored the plight of the Confederacy under his leadership. "Where is this to end?" Gorgas wondered. "No money in the Treasury, no food to feed General Lee's Army, no troops to oppose Gen. Sherman. . . . Is the cause really hopeless? Is it to be abandoned and lost in this way? . . . When I see the President trifle away precious hours [in] idle discussion & discursive comment, I feel as tho' he were not equal to his great task. And yet where could we get a better or a wiser man?"[5]

Many believed that a wiser and better man was available: General Robert E. Lee. Pressure mounted on Davis to appoint Lee as general-in-chief with virtually dictatorial powers that would, in effect, usurp the president's authority as commander in chief. Davis likewise faced demands for the restoration of

Johnston to command of the remnants of the Army of Tennessee. Mixed with these pressures were a welter of rumors and speculations about a wholesale reshuffling of the cabinet, the resignation of Davis, even a coup d'état to remove him from office. "There are rumors of revolution, and even of the displacement of the President by Congress, and investiture of Gen. Lee," recorded one diarist breathlessly. "Revolution, the deposition of Mr. Davis, is openly talked of!" reported another.[6]

In the midst of this ferment came news of the fall of Fort Fisher on January 15, which closed Wilmington, North Carolina, as the last port for blockade runners bringing supplies for Lee's army. As the noose tightened around the Confederacy's neck, on January 16 the Senate overwhelmingly passed a resolution calling for the appointment of Lee as general-in-chief. The Virginia legislature sent Davis a similar resolution the following day. The president adroitly replied that he too had great confidence in Lee and was quite willing to give him command of all Confederate armies if Lee thought it compatible with his duties as field commander of the Army of Northern Virginia. The same day Davis offered Lee the position, knowing that he would decline, thus taking some of the sting out of the passage by the House that day of a bill creating the position of general-in-chief. A War Department official declared that the bill "is very distasteful to the President." But "it is a question whether he will have the hardihood to veto it."[7] Davis signed it, however, and named Lee to the post on February 1. This time the general reluctantly accepted, with the apparent understanding that he would exercise his powers minimally, without infringing on the president's prerogatives as commander in chief.[8]

THIS DENOUEMENT TEMPORARILY LANCED THE BOIL OF DIS-sension in Richmond. At the same time, the issue of negotiations to bring the war to an end was coming to a head. Ever since Abraham Lincoln's reelection in November, the North's purpose to fight on to victory or exhaustion was clear. And it was also clear that the side closest to exhaustion was the Confederacy. Inflation and shortages had destroyed its economy; its armies were reeling in defeat; desertions had become epidemic; malnutrition and depressed morale prevailed among soldiers and civilians alike. A longing for peace spread over the South. A supporter of Davis told him in January that "making all proper allowances for habitual croakers, & personal dissatisfactions, I must express the deliberate conviction that there exists now an amount of conflict & despondency, which threatens to disintegrate & destroy our Government. Day by day things are growing worse."[9] The Georgia and Alabama legislatures passed resolutions calling for negotiations. Several congressmen introduced similar resolutions. Vice President Alexander Stephens once again pressed Davis to pursue any possible avenue toward peace.[10]

Davis had no faith in such a pursuit. He knew that Lincoln would insist on reunion and emancipation as the sine qua nons of peace. Davis continued to insist that the Confederacy could achieve independence by outlasting the North's willingness to continue fighting. But he could not ignore the pressure for negotiations. He must at least appear willing to explore any opportunity for peace.

Such an opportunity opened up in the form of a letter from Francis Preston Blair at the beginning of 1865. A prominent Jacksonian Democrat during the 1830s and 1840s, Blair had been a political ally and friend of Davis's. They had parted company when Blair helped found the Republican Party and became a sort of elder statesman in the Lincoln administration. He persuaded Lincoln to allow him to go to Richmond under a flag of truce as a "wholly unaccredited" agent to seek an interview with his old friend in the Confederate White House. The ostensible purpose was to obtain the return of papers looted by Confederate soldiers from Blair's home in Silver Spring, Maryland, when Maj. Gen. Jubal Early's Confederate troops raided to the outskirts of Washington the previous July. The real purpose, conveyed in a private letter to Davis, was to see if they could find common ground to end the war.[11]

Davis and Blair met for several hours in Richmond on January 12. Blair presented his personal plan for peace: a cease-fire between Union and Confederate forces followed by an alliance to drive the French out of Mexico, where Louis Napoleon had installed Austrian archduke Ferdinand Maximilian as emperor. Davis was skeptical about this audacious scheme, but he did not rule it out. The two men agreed to disagree, however, on the nature of such an alliance: Blair saw it as a step toward the return of the South to the Union; Davis perceived it as an agreement between two nations. Davis gave Blair a letter for Lincoln in which he agreed to appoint commissioners to a meeting with Union commissioners "with a view to secure peace to the two countries."[12]

Blair went back to Washington with this message. Lincoln had no interest in Blair's Mexican adventure. But he too wanted to keep alive the chance for peace. He authorized Blair to return to Richmond with a letter offering to receive any agents Davis "may informally send to me, with the view of securing peace to the people of our one common country."[13] After meetings with his cabinet and with Vice President Stephens, Davis decided to send a commission despite the difference between "the two countries" and "our one common country."

Stephens had been one of the president's most persistent critics, and to get him off his back Davis named him one of the three commissioners. The others were Assistant Secretary of War John A. Campbell, a former U.S. Supreme Court justice, and Senator Robert M. T. Hunter of Virginia. All three had urged negotiations; Davis was sure that the process would founder on the one country/two countries impasse, so he wanted his commissioners to be personal witnesses to Lincoln's "intransigence" as a way to convince the Southern people that independence could be achieved only by military victory.[14]

Davis asked Secretary of State Judah Benjamin to draft instructions to the commissioners. Benjamin fudged the difference between one country and two countries by referring to Davis's offer to negotiate and instructing them to seek a conference with Union agents "upon the subject to which it relates." That would never do, said Davis. He restored "the two countries"

Alexander H. Stephens

language in the instructions. Benjamin shook his head and predicted that "the whole thing will break down on that very point."[15]

If it had not been for the intervention of General Ulysses S. Grant, it would indeed have broken down. Lincoln had ordered Union officers not to allow the commissioners to cross the lines unless they agreed to his "one common country" letter as the basis for a meeting. Davis's "two countries" instructions seemed to preclude a conference. By this time, however, the press in both North and South was full of speculation about the prospect of peace. The failure of the commissioners at least to meet would produce a huge letdown. Grant talked informally with Stephens and Hunter and telegraphed the War Department that he believed "their intentions are good and their desire sincere to restore peace and union. . . . I am sorry however that Mr. Lincoln cannot have an interview with [them]. . . . I fear now their going back without any expression from anyone in authority will have a bad influence."[16]

This telegram caused Lincoln to come personally to Fort Monroe, where he joined Secretary of State William H. Seward for a meeting with the three Confederate commissioners on February 3. The four-hour meeting on a boat at Hampton Roads produced just what Davis expected—and probably wanted. Lincoln insisted on three conditions for peace: "1 The restoration of the National authority throughout all the States. 2 No receding by the Executive of the United States, on the Slavery question. . . . 3 No cessation of hostilities short of an end of the war, and the disbanding of all forces hostile to the government."[17]

Three days earlier the United States Congress had passed—and Lincoln had signed—the Thirteenth Amendment to the Constitution abolishing slavery, so condition number 2 would mean the end of the South's peculiar institution.

The commissioners had no authority to accept any of these conditions, so they went home empty-handed. Their report to Davis contained only a bare-bones summary of the discussion. Davis, in order to fire up Southern resentment and determination to resist, wanted them to add some words about Lincoln's insistence on humiliating terms. They refused, so on February 6 Davis provided such language in his message sending the report to Congress, which he also released to the press. Lincoln offered only the terms of a "conqueror," he declared, demanding "unconditional submission to their rule."[18]

That evening and three nights later Davis rose from a sick-bed to give defiant speeches at mass meetings called to rally Southern morale. The Confederacy must fight on and prevail, he declared. It could never submit to the "disgrace of surrender" to "His Majesty Abraham the First." Instead, Lincoln and Seward would find that "they had been speaking to their masters," for Southern armies would yet "compel the Yankees, in less than twelve months, to petition us for peace on our own terms."[19] Even Davis's critics praised these speeches. The editor of the *Richmond Examiner* admitted that he had never been "so much moved by the power of words." Alexander Stephens thought Davis's performance was "brilliant," though he regarded the president's forecast of military victory as "the emanation of a demented brain."[20]

These meetings succeeded in reviving enthusiasm for the war, at least in Richmond. "Never before has the war spirit burned so fiercely and steadily," exclaimed the *Richmond Dispatch,* while Josiah Gorgas echoed: "The war spirit has blazed out afresh." The War Department clerk John B. Jones recorded that "every one thinks that the Confederacy will at once gather up its military strength and strike such blows as will astonish the world."[21]

Several changes in the management of the war reinforced this optimism. Lee became general-in-chief at this time. James Seddon, worn out and in ill health, resigned as secretary of war and was replaced by John C. Breckinridge, who infused new energy into the War Department. One of Breckinridge's first actions was to persuade Davis to accept the resignation of the much-maligned Lucius Northrop as commissary general and to appoint the able Isaac St. John in his place. The meager flow of rations to Lee's army soon improved.[22]

But the euphoria in Richmond wore off as Sherman headed north from Savannah with the obvious purpose of cutting a destructive swath through the Carolinas and coming up on Lee's rear in Virginia while Grant held him in a viselike grip in front. Charleston fell on February 18, when Sherman cut its communications with the interior. These developments increased the already intense pressure on Davis to restore Johnston to command of the forces concentrating in North Carolina to try to stop Sherman. Howell Cobb implored the president to "respond to the urgent—overwhelming public feeling in favor of the restoration of Genl Johnston. . . . Better that you put him in command— admitting him to be as deficient in the qualities of a General—

as you or anyone else may suppose—than to resist a public sentiment—which is weakening your strength—and destroying your powers of usefulness." Another Davis supporter acknowledged that the president had been justified in removing Johnston, but now it was necessary to reappoint him. "It would be equal to [the addition of] more than ten thousand effective men to the army. I entreat you, Mr. President, refuse no longer."[23]

War Department clerk John Jones succinctly expressed Davis's dilemma in the face of this pressure: "What will the President *do,* after *saying* [Johnston] should never have another command?" What Davis did was to produce a long memorandum, dated February 18, detailing his perception of all of Johnston's failures and deficiencies. He intended to send it to Congress in response to resolutions by both houses calling for Johnston's reappointment.[24] But he did not send it. Instead, four days later he swallowed the bitter pill and named Johnston to the command. It was Lee who persuaded him to do so, by suggesting the fig leaf that Johnston be ordered "to report to me." This was Lee's one real exercise of authority as general-in-chief. "I know of no one who has so much the confidence of the troops & people as Genl Johnston," Lee told Davis, "and I shall do all in my power to strengthen him."[25]

IT WAS BEYOND LEE'S POWER TO STRENGTHEN JOHNSTON with significant reinforcements. Johnston could scrape together scarcely 20,000 effective men to confront Sherman's 60,000,

while in Virginia Lee had fewer than 60,000 to challenge
Grant's 125,000. Both Confederate armies were suffering an
epidemic of desertions and absences without leave. Davis deplored this leakage, which was draining the Confederacy's life-
blood. But many generals blamed the president himself for
failing to uphold the summary executions of deserters that
would discourage others from taking off. Like Lincoln, Davis
pardoned or commuted the death sentences of many deserters.
He hoped that clemency and an appeal to patriotism would
work better than savage discipline in making men willing to
fight. But this strategy did not seem to be working. And it led
to one of Davis's rare conflicts with Lee, who complained of the
laxity that encouraged desertion. "I think a rigid execution of
the law is mercy in the end," wrote Lee. "The great want in our
army is firm discipline." Davis penned a biting commentary on
Lee's complaint. If the commander in chief saw fit to exercise
clemency, he wrote, "that is not a proper subject for the criticism of a military commander."[26]

The fact remained, however, that the Confederacy faced an
acute manpower crisis in early 1865. Its armies had only 126,000
men present for duty of a total of 359,000 on its rolls. (At the
same time, Union armies had 621,000 present of a total of
959,000 on the rolls.)[27] In this dire state of affairs, many were
prepared to consider what had previously been unthinkable—the
freeing and enlisting of slaves as soldiers in the Confederate army.

Of course, slaves had always been an essential part of Confederate armies as laborers, teamsters, hospital attendants, laun-
dresses, servants, cooks, and so on. In a message to Congress on

November 27, 1863, Davis had recommended legislation to increase their number in order to release for combat many white soldiers serving in those capacities. Congress had complied; it had also repealed the draftee's privilege of hiring a substitute and ended many occupational exemptions.[28]

These measures, however, failed to live up to their potential for increasing the number of combat soldiers. As early as July 1863, Davis began hearing from constituents suggesting the use of slaves as soldiers.[29] A few Southern newspapers urged consideration of this radical idea. "We are forced by the necessity of our condition . . . to take a step which is revolting to every sentiment of pride, and to every principle that governed our institutions before the war," declared an editor in Montgomery, Alabama, in the fall of 1863. An editor in Mobile, Alabama, concurred: "It is better for us to use the negroes for our defense than that the Yankees should use them against us. . . . We can make them fight better than the Yankees are able to do. Masters and overseers can marshal them for battle by the same authority and habit of obedience with which they are marshalled to labor."[30]

Such ideas were anathema to most Confederates at that time, including Davis. When the proposal came from a significant source within the army itself, the president suppressed it. In January 1864 the best division commander in the Army of Tennessee, Maj. Gen. Patrick Cleburne, presented a paper to his fellow officers at the army's winter camp in Dalton, Georgia. The North was winning the war, wrote Cleburne, because of its greater resources and manpower, including the freed slaves it was recruiting into the Union army. "Slavery, from being one of our chief sources of strength at the commencement of the war, has now become, in a military point of view, one of our chief sources of weakness." Thus the Confederacy was threatened with "the loss of all we now hold most sacred—slaves and all other personal property, lands, homesteads, liberty, justice, safety, pride, manhood." To avoid this disaster, said Cleburne, the Confederacy should enlist its own slave soldiers and "guarantee freedom within a reasonable time to every slave in the South who shall remain true to the Confederacy."[31]

Thirteen brigadier generals and other officers in Cleburne's division signed this paper. But officers in other units condemned the "monstrous proposition" as "revolting to Southern sentiment, Southern pride, and Southern honor."[32] One division commander was so upset that he went out of channels and sent a copy to Davis with a request that he crack down on "the further agitation of such sentiments and propositions," which "would ruin the efficiency of our Army and involve our cause in ruin and disgrace." The governor-in-exile of Tennessee urged Davis to "smother" the proposal so that it did not "gain publicity."[33] Davis agreed, and ordered Johnston to destroy all copies. "If it be kept out of the public journals," he wrote, "its ill effects will be much lessened." So successful was the "smothering" that Cleburne's paper remained unknown outside a small circle until 1890, when one copy saved by a member of Cleburne's staff turned up during the publication of the official records of the war.[34]

The issue of slave soldiers remained muted during most of

1864. But the manpower crisis in the collapsing Confederacy revived it by November. Davis approached the matter gingerly in a message to Congress on November 7. He recommended the appropriation of funds (where the money would come from he did not say) for the purchase of forty thousand slaves to be employed in noncombat roles by the army and freed after "service faithfully rendered." He did not think it "wise or advantageous" to arm them as soldiers, he said before inserting a bombshell sentence: "But should the alternative ever be presented of subjugation or of the employment of the slave as a soldier, there seems no reason to doubt what should then be our decision."[35]

No one missed the import of these words. "Can one credit it?" wrote a North Carolina woman who opposed the emancipation feature as well as the implied endorsement of black soldiers. "That a Southern man, one who knows the evils of free negroism, can be found willing to inflict such a curse on his country? . . . I consider such conduct undignified & unworthy of Mr. Davis, for that he really advocates the measure I cannot and will not believe."[36] The usual suspects among Davis's most bitter critics, the *Richmond Examiner* and the *Charleston Mercury,* weighed in against the president's proposal. "It adopts the whole theory of the abolitionist," declared the *Examiner.* "The existence of a negro soldier is totally inconsistent with our political aim and with our social as well as political system. . . . If a negro is fit to be a soldier he is not fit to be a slave. . . . It would be a confession, not only of weakness, but of absolute inability to secure the object for which we undertook the war." The *Mercury* branded Davis's proposition as "inconsistent, unsound, and suicidal. . . . It would give the lie to our professions and surrender the strength and power of our position."[37]

Congress did not act on Davis's recommendation to buy and free 40,000 slaves "after service faithfully rendered." But as the Confederacy's prospects grew worse over the winter of 1864–65, the idea of arming the slaves would not die. A planter in North Carolina who owned 125 slaves offered 50 of them to Davis for the army. "I will pledge my word and judgment they will fight as well as the neg[ro] in the northern army. . . . We are on the verge of ruin unless this last resort is brought to bear." A Georgia planter who had lost two sons in the war believed the time had come to enlist black soldiers. "We should away with pride of opinion—away with false pride," he wrote to Davis. "The enemy fights us with the negro—and they will do very well to fight the yankees. . . . We are reduced to the last resort."[38]

By February 1865 Davis was willing to commit openly to the last resort. In a letter to the editor of the influential *Mobile Advertiser and Register,* which supported this policy, the president expressed approval of "employing for the defence of our Country all the able-bodied men we have without distinction of color. . . . We are reduced to choosing whether the negroes shall fight for or against us."[39]

As the balance of opinion seemed to shift toward this position, the opposition became more shrill. "No question has arisen during the war that has given me so much concern," Senator David Yulee of Florida told Davis. "This is a White Man's government. To associate the colors in camp is to unsettle castes; and when thereby the distinction of color and caste is so far

Howell Cobb

obliterated that the relation of fellow soldier is accepted, the mixture of races, and toleration of equality, is commenced." Howell Cobb let the president know his opinion that "the proposition to make soldiers of our slaves [is] the most pernicious idea that has been suggested since the war began. . . . If slaves will make good soldiers—our whole theory of slavery is wrong."[40] Some white Southerners apparently preferred to lose the war than to win it with the help of black men. "Victory itself would be robbed of its glory if shared with slaves," declared a Mississippi congressman. President Davis's chief nemesis, Senator Louis Wigfall, said that he "wanted to live in no country in which the man who blacked his boots and curried his horse was his equal."[41]

A bill introduced in Congress on February 10 for black enlistments therefore faced rough sledding in spite of Davis's support—perhaps in part *because* of that support. Sponsored by Representative Ethelbert Barksdale of Mississippi (whose brother had been killed at Gettysburg), it authorized the president to requisition a quota of black soldiers from each state, with consent of their owners, but said nothing about freeing them. The House passed this measure by a vote of 40–37, but the Senate defeated it by one vote, 11–10, with both Virginia senators voting no. Meanwhile, Robert E. Lee came out publicly for the bill. Lee had earlier told a Virginia state senator in private that he favored the use of slaves as soldiers. On February 18 he made public his belief that such a policy was "not only expedient but necessary. . . . The negroes, under proper circumstances, will make efficient soldiers. I think we could do at least as well with them as the enemy, and he attaches great importance to their assistance. . . . Those who are employed should be freed. It would be neither just nor wise . . . to require them to serve as slaves."[42]

Lee's intervention proved decisive. The Virginia legislature instructed the state's senators to change their votes to yes. They did so reluctantly, enabling the bill to pass by a vote of 9–8 (with nine abstentions and absences). Davis quickly signed it into law on March 13. The measure did not confer freedom on those who enlisted. But Davis ordered the War Department to issue regulations that ensured them "the rights of a freedman."[43] The president tried to jump-start the recruitment of black regiments. But the effort was too little and too late. Two companies began organizing in Richmond, but before this process got very far, the city fell on April 2 and the war was soon over.[44]

While the glare of publicity focused on the controversy over black soldiers, Davis and Secretary of State Judah Benjamin inaugurated a secret diplomatic mission to offer gradual abolition of slavery in return for British and French recognition of the Confederacy. The initiative for this mission came from Duncan F. Kenner, a wealthy sugar planter from Louisiana and a prominent member of the Confederate Congress. Kenner had been convinced since the fall of New Orleans in 1862 that slavery was a millstone around the Confederacy's neck. He had urged Davis to consider an emancipationist diplomacy, but he made no headway until December 1864, when the president asked him to undertake such a mission. Davis of course could not commit Congress to an abolition policy, nor could Congress commit the states. But perhaps the Europeans would overlook these technicalities. Judah Benjamin convinced Davis that he could invoke his war powers to proclaim emancipation as a military necessity for national survival. When Lincoln had justified *his* Emancipation Proclamation on similar grounds in January 1863, Davis had denounced it as "the most execrable measure recorded in the history of guilty man." But that was then, and this was now.[45]

Kenner's difficulties in getting to Europe foretokened the failure of his mission. Because of the fall of Fort Fisher, he could not take a blockade runner from Wilmington. He traveled incognito to New York and boarded a ship to France, where Louis Napoleon gave him a cold shoulder. His experience in Britain was no better. On March 14 Lord Palmerston informed Kenner and the Confederate envoy James Mason, who had accompanied him to London, that the British government could not recognize a nation that had not firmly established its existence. "As affairs now stood," Mason reported to Benjamin, "our seaports given up, the comparatively unobstructed march of Sherman, etc., rather increased than diminished previous objections."[46]

By March 1865 the Confederacy was falling apart. The railroads had broken down and could scarcely move the little freight that the inflation-ravaged economy produced. Deserters roamed the countryside and robbed civilians of what little sustenance they had preserved. Government officials, including President Davis, sent their families away from Richmond

J. C. Breckinridge

because of the prospect of its imminent fall. A clerical worker in the War Department wrote in her diary on March 10: "Fearful orders have been given in the offices to keep the papers packed, except such as we are working on. The packed boxes remain in the front room. . . . As we walk in every morning, all eyes are turned to the boxes to see if any have been removed, and we breathe more freely when we find them still there."[47]

When John C. Breckinridge became secretary of war in February, he ordered a survey of Confederate resources available to carry on the war. The results were shocking: no money; no credit; shortages of food, clothing, forage, munitions, animals, and men; no more foreign imports because of the fall of Wilmington. Breckinridge and Assistant Secretary of War John A. Campbell were convinced that the war was lost and that the government should negotiate a peace even with reunion while it still had leverage to salvage something from the ruin. They approached Lee, who agreed that matters were almost hopeless. But Lee—and for that matter Breckinridge—refused to defy the president so long as Davis was determined to fight on. Lee emerged from a meeting with Davis impressed by his "remarkable faith" in the cause and his "unconquerable will power." The general told a Virginia congressman that as long as the war continued he would fight "to the last extremity."[48]

In Davis's mind, that last extremity had not arrived. "There are no vital points on the preservation of which the continued existence of the Confederacy depends," he had told Congress in November 1864. "Not the fall of Richmond, nor Wilmington, nor Charleston, nor Savannah, nor Mobile, nor of all combined, can save the enemy from the constant and exhaustive drain of blood and treasure which must continue until he shall discover that no peace is attainable unless based on the recognition of our indefeasible rights."[49]

By the beginning of March 1865 three of those cities had fallen and the other two would soon follow. A Senate committee asked Davis what he intended to do. According to the committee's report, the president told them that he meant "to continue the war as long as we were able to maintain it. . . . The existence of the Confederate Government was a fact, and that he was placed in office to defend and preserve it, that he had power to negotiate for the continued existence of the Government, but none whatever for its destruction."[50]

Davis liked to cite the example of Frederick the Great, who faced a powerful coalition that greatly outnumbered him in the Seven Years' War but attacked and defeated his enemies in detail and saved Silesia for Prussia. He had this example in mind when he wrote to Braxton Bragg on April 1 that "our condition is that in which great Generals have shown their value to a struggling state. Boldness of conception and rapidity of execution has often rendered the smaller force victorious. To fight the Enemy in detail it is necessary to outmarch him and to surprise him."[51]

It was not to be. While attending Sunday service at St. Paul's Church the next day, Davis was handed an urgent message from Lee. The enemy had broken the lines at Petersburg, and the capital must be evacuated. That night Davis and his cabinet boarded the last train from Richmond as the city, its warehouses

*Petersburg, Virginia: Dead Confederate soldiers
in the trenches of Fort Mahone*

set afire by departing Confederate troops, began to burn behind them. Davis's destination was Danville, Virginia, the new
Confederate capital. From there on April 4 he issued a proclamation to the Southern people urging them to continue the struggle. "Relieved from the necessity of guarding cities and particular
points," he declared, the army would be "free to move from
point to point, and strike in detail the detachments and garrisons of the enemy, operating in the interior of our own country,
where supplies are accessible. . . . Nothing is now needed to render our triumph certain, but the exhibition of our own unquenchable resolve. Let us but will it, and we are free."[52]

Because of the breakdown in communications, few people
read this appeal and fewer heeded it. After a week in Danville
the cabinet learned of Lee's surrender at Appomattox. They
hastily fled south to Greensboro, North Carolina. Joseph Johnston's small army was still in the field, near Raleigh, and Davis
hoped to use it as a nucleus to build up a larger force to continue the war. "We must redouble our efforts to meet present
disaster," he told North Carolina's governor, Zebulon Vance.
"An army holding its position with determination to fight on
and manifest ability to maintain the struggle will attract all the
scattered soldiers and daily and rapidly gather strength."[53]

Davis had gone from a state of unreality to one of fantasy.
"Poor President," commented a Confederate soldier. "He is un-
willing to see what all around him see. He cannot bring himself
to believe that after four years of glorious struggle we are to
be crushed into submission."[54] Johnston's army surrendered to
Sherman on April 26. Davis continued south, two steps ahead

Richmond, Virginia: Ruins on Carey Street

DAVIS'S FLIGHT FROM RICHMOND, APRIL 2–MAY 10, 1865

of Union cavalry scouring the countryside looking for him. One by one his cabinet members resigned, but he hoped to make his way across the Mississippi River to join Edmund Kirby Smith's troops, who had not yet surrendered. On May 10, however, Union cavalry caught up with his small party, including his family, near Irwinville, Georgia.

The long ordeal of civil war was over. For Davis there began a new ordeal of imprisonment for two years awaiting a trial for treason that never came. Twenty-four years of a long life remained during which he never recanted the cause for which he had fought and lost.

CODA

Where could we get a better or a wiser man" than Jefferson Davis for commander in chief? wondered Josiah Gorgas in 1865. There was of course no right or wrong answer to that question. Nobody can say whether Robert Toombs, Howell Cobb, or any other potential Confederate president would have been more successful. What we do know about those gentlemen elicits skepticism. Most delegates to the Montgomery convention in 1861 believed Davis to be the best man for the job, and no clear evidence exists that they were wrong. The fact that the Confederacy lost the war does not prove that it could have been won with a different commander in chief. And under Davis's leadership, the South appeared to be on the cusp of success on at least three occasions when Confederate victories had caused deep demoralization in the North: the summer of 1862, the winter and spring of 1863, and the summer of 1864. But Union victories at Antietam, Vicksburg, Gettysburg, and Atlanta blunted Southern momentum and revived Northern determination to fight through to ultimate triumph.

Could Jefferson Davis have done anything different on those three occasions or at any other time during the war to produce Confederate victory? That question too is ultimately unanswerable, but this has not stopped historians from speculating. Such speculation focuses mainly on two subjects: military strategy and military commanders. Would a different strategy have brought Confederate success? The political necessity to defend all frontiers of the Confederacy produced a strategy of dispersed defense in 1861. Davis would have preferred a strategy of concentration for an offensive-defensive campaign (as he termed it), but demands from state governors and other officials required dispersion. The initial poverty of weapons and logistical capacity precluded large offensives.

Union success in breaking through the thin gray lines of dispersed defenses in 1862 forced a revision of Confederate strategy. With new commanders of the two principal Southern armies, Robert E. Lee and Braxton Bragg, the Confederates embarked on their most ambitious offensive-defensive campaigns in the late summer of 1862, with a reprise in Pennsylvania in the summer of 1863. After experiencing initial success, these campaigns ultimately failed. Subsequent Union offensives compelled the Confederacy to fall back to an essentially defensive strategy for the rest of the war.

The two principal exceptions to that defensive strategy were

Jubal Early's raid to the outskirts of Washington in July 1864 and John Bell Hood's invasion of Tennessee in November. They resulted in the virtual destruction of these two Southern armies in the Shenandoah Valley in October and at Nashville in December. These two campaigns were clearly beyond the Confederates' capacity to execute by that stage of the war. Lee's prosecution of offensive-defensive operations in 1862 and 1863 may have represented the Confederacy's best chance for victory, but Hood's effort to repeat that strategy in 1864 was wrongheaded, and Davis's approval of that invasion may have been his worst strategic mistake.

Two other options were available to the Confederacy. The first was a "Fabian" strategy of yielding territory to the enemy until the moment came to strike at his most vulnerable tentacles. Like the Roman general Quintus Fabius in the Second Punic War, or George Washington in the American Revolution, or the Russian general Mikhail Kutuzov in 1812, Confederate commanders could have traded space for time, kept the army concentrated and ready to strike enemy detachments dangling deep in Southern territory, and above all avoided destruction of their armies. Such a Fabian defensive strategy, so the argument goes, might have worn out the will or capacity of the Union to continue fighting, as the Americans and Russians had done to the British and French in 1781 and 1812–13. To a considerable degree, this was Joseph Johnston's apparent strategy in Virginia in 1862 and especially in Georgia in 1864. But Johnston seemed prepared to yield Richmond and Atlanta rather than risk his army—and he did stand by while Vicksburg fell.

To Davis this was a strategy of surrender that would have had fatal consequences for the Confederacy. He was probably right. In the end the strategy of the offensive-defensive did not work either, but as practiced by Robert E. Lee it probably came closest to success.

Another strategic alternative was guerrilla war. Confederate partisans were active behind Union lines in several theaters, and quasi-guerrilla cavalry commanders like Nathan Bedford Forrest and John Hunt Morgan also carried out many successful raids. Although Davis approved of these activities, he showed relatively little interest in guerrilla warfare as a primary strategy. In this lack of interest his instincts were probably sound. The Confederacy was an established polity with the institutions of a nation-state and an organized army with professional commanders. Conventional warfare supplemented by auxiliary guerrilla operations or cavalry raids behind enemy lines represented its best strategic mix. Guerrilla actions as the main strategy are most appropriate for a rebel force trying to *capture* the institutions of government, not to defend them. And a slave society that practices guerrilla warfare is playing with fire, for it opens up opportunities for the slaves to carry out their own guerrilla actions against the regime.

Most critical appraisals of Davis as commander in chief have focused more on his choices of generals and his relations with them than on his choice of strategies. Davis's alleged favoritism toward old West Point classmates and army comrades like Theophilus Holmes, Leonidas Polk, and Lucius Northrop has been the subject of much censure. His high regard for Albert

Sidney Johnston, Braxton Bragg, John C. Pemberton, and John Bell Hood, which caused him to appoint them to top commands where they failed to measure up to expectations, likewise raised questions about his judgment. Davis's supposed vendettas against two of the Confederacy's foremost generals, Pierre G. T. Beauregard and Joseph E. Johnston, have generated reams of reproach. His stubborn insistence on retaining Northrop, Holmes, Polk, and Bragg in their posts despite widespread criticism alienated many people and weakened his administration. Beauregard and especially Joseph Johnston became the focal points of an increasingly corrosive political opposition that undermined Davis's ability to lead.

Some of these negative appraisals are at least partly justified. Northrop, Holmes, Polk, and perhaps Pemberton did not deserve Davis's high opinion of their merits. His continued support for them did evince favoritism. His faith in Hood may have been misplaced. The issue of Braxton Bragg is more complicated. Davis recognized that part of the opposition to Bragg by his principal subordinates was petty and self-serving. And he did try to get Joseph Johnston to replace Bragg in the spring of 1863, when it became clear that Bragg had lost the confidence of his senior generals. But Johnston managed to evade the responsibility. Davis then tried twice to persuade Robert E. Lee to take this troubled command, but Lee also demurred. Either Beauregard or Johnston probably would have accepted command of the Army of Tennessee after the next outbreak of an anti-Bragg revolt following Chickamauga, and Davis probably should have appointed one of them.

His refusal to do so raises the matter of his caustic relationships with these two top generals. It seems clear that in both cases Davis was more sinned against than sinning. Beauregard's outsize ego caused him repeatedly to glorify himself at Davis's expense. The president should perhaps have given Beauregard more slack, but his distrust of the general was surely justified. As for Johnston, Davis showed heroic patience with that general's constant complaints, frequent flouting of presidential orders, and failure to keep Davis informed of his operational plans. The president gave Johnston *more* slack than he deserved. Davis's most controversial act, the removal of Johnston from command in July 1864, was fully warranted. The military historian Richard McMurry was not being entirely facetious when he said, in a casual conversation, that if Johnston had been left in command he would have fought the crucial battle of the Atlanta campaign at Key West.

Davis's relationship with General Robert E. Lee was one of the brightest features of his tenure as commander in chief. The president recognized Lee's ability and supported the general in the face of initial criticisms. The two men forged a partnership even closer and longer lasting than the one between Lincoln and Grant on the other side. And while the Lincoln-Grant team eventually won the war, this does not mean that the Davis-Lee team was responsible for losing it. For in the final analysis, the salient truth about the American Civil War is not that the Confederacy lost but that the Union won.

ACKNOWLEDGMENTS

I could not have written this book without the pioneering scholarship of William J. Cooper, Jr., and William C. "Jack" Davis, whose biographies of Jefferson Davis provided much of the framework for my own research. That research was made possible by the professionalism of Lynda Lasswell Crist and her fellow editors of *The Papers of Jefferson Davis* at Rice University, whose scholarly thoroughness provided me with access to all known documentation on Davis as commander in chief, supplementing the earlier edition of Davis's speeches, letters, and telegrams edited in the 1920s by Dunbar Rowland.

I am grateful to Scott Moyers of The Penguin Press for suggesting that I undertake this project and for keeping faith in it from first to last. Copy editor Adam Goldberger improved the accuracy and readability of my prose, while Mally Anderson and production editor Bruce Giffords shepherded the manuscript through the process of publication. Bill Nelson skillfully drew the maps. To all of them I owe a big vote of thanks.

ACKNOWLEDGMENTS

My wife, Patricia McPherson, tolerated my preoccupation with Jefferson Davis, who is not her favorite historical character. But she recognizes that we cannot understand the Civil War and its meaning without coming to grips with the Confederate as well as the Union commander in chief.

NOTES

Abbreviations

Crist, *PJD*, followed by volume and page numbers, for Lynda Lasswell Crist, Mary Seaton Dix, Kenneth H. Williams, Barbara J. Rozek, and Peggy L. Dillard, eds., *The Papers of Jefferson Davis,* vols. 7–11 (Baton Rouge: Louisiana State University Press, 1992–2003).

O.R., followed by series, volume, part, and page numbers, for *The War of the Rebellion: A Compilation of the Official Records of the Union and Confederate Armies,* 70 volumes in 128 serials (Washington, D.C.: Government Printing Office, 1880–1901).

Rowland, *JDC,* followed by volume and page numbers, for Dunbar Rowland, ed., *Jefferson Davis, Constitutionalist: His Letters, Papers and Speeches,* vols. 5–6 (Jackson: Mississippi Department of Archives and History, 1923).

Introduction

1. *Personal Memoirs of U. S. Grant,* 2 vols. (New York: Charles L. Webster, 1885–86), 2:87; David M. Potter, "Jefferson Davis and the Political Factors in Confederate Defeat," in David Donald, ed., *Why the North Won the Civil War* (Baton Rouge: Louisiana State University Press, 1960), 102, 112.

2. James M. McPherson, *Tried by War: Abraham Lincoln as Commander in Chief* (New York: Penguin Press, 2008).

3. George Bagby, quoted in Emory M. Thomas, *The Confederate Nation, 1861–1865* (New York: Harper & Row, 1979), 142.

4. Quoted in E. Merton Coulter, *The Confederate States of America 1861–1865* (Baton Rouge: Louisiana State University Press, 1950), 385–86.

5. James Z. Rabun, "Alexander H. Stephens and Jefferson Davis," *American Historical Review* 58 (1953): 307.

6. Quoted in T. Michael Parrish, "Jeff Davis Rules: General Beauregard and the Sanctity of Civilian Authority in the Confederacy," in Gabor S. Boritt, ed., *Jefferson Davis's Generals* (New York: Oxford University Press, 1999), 38.

7. Stephen R. Mallory to his son "Buddy," Sept. 27, 1865, in Joseph T. Durkin, *Stephen R. Mallory: Confederate Navy Chief* (Chapel Hill: University of North Carolina Press, 1954), 179.

8. George Akin, quoted in Grady McWhiney, "Jefferson Davis and His Generals," in McWhiney, *Southerners and Other Americans* (New York: Basic Books, 1973), 85–86. See also Crist, *PJD,* 11:299.

9. Harris D. Riley, Jr., "Jefferson Davis and His Health," *Journal of Mississippi History* 49 (1987): 179–202, 262–87.

10. John B. Jones, *A Rebel War Clerk's Diary at the Confederate States Capital,* ed. Howard Swiggett, 2 vols. (New York: Old Hickory Bookshop, 1935), 1:312, 319, entries of May 6 and 19, 1863.

11. Gary Gallagher, *The Confederate War* (Cambridge, Mass.: Harvard University Press, 1997).

1. WE MUST PREPARE FOR A LONG WAR

1. Varina Howell Davis, *Jefferson Davis, Ex-President of the Confederate States of America: A Memoir by His Wife,* 2 vols. (New York: Belford, 1890), 2:18–19; Jefferson Davis to Alexander M. Clayton, Jan. 30, 1861, Davis to Franklin Stringfellow, June 4, 1878, Crist, *PJD,* 7:28, 29n.

2. Davis to Francis Pickens, Feb. 20, 1861, Crist, *PJD,* 7:55.

3. *New Orleans Delta,* Feb. 14, 1861, quoted in William C. Davis, *Jefferson Davis: The Man and His Hour* (New York: HarperCollins, 1991), 305; *Memphis Daily Appeal,* Feb. 19, 1861, Crist, *PJD,* 7:42.

4. *Charleston Tri-Weekly Mercury,* Feb. 19, 1861, in Rowland, *JDC,* 5:48; Davis's address, ibid., 5:49–53.

5. Davis to Semmes, Feb. 21, 1861, ibid., 5:54–56.

6. T. Harry Williams, *P. G. T. Beauregard: Napoleon in Gray* (Baton Rouge: Louisiana State University Press, 1955), 49–50; Grady McWhiney, *Braxton Bragg and Confederate Defeat* (New York: Columbia University Press, 1969), 167; Davis to Pickens, Feb. 22, 1861, Davis to Braxton Bragg, Apr. 3, 1861, Crist, *PJD,* 7:57, 85–86; Davis to Pickens, Mar. 1, 1861, Rowland, *JDC,* 5:58–59.

7. Davis to Bragg, Apr. 3, 1861, Crist, *PJD,* 7:85–86.

8. W. C. Davis, *Davis,* 320–23; William J. Cooper, *Jefferson Davis, American* (New York: Alfred A. Knopf, 2000), 337–40; Herman Hattaway and Richard E. Beringer, *Jefferson Davis, Confederate President* (Lawrence: University Press of Kansas, 2002), 65–66; Rowland, *JDC,* 5:97–98.

9. Charlotte Maria Wigfall to Louise Wigfall, Apr. 26, 1861, in Louise Wigfall, *A Southern Girl in '61: The Wartime Memories of a Confederate Senator's Daughter* (New York: Doubleday, Page, 1905), 49.

10. C. Vann Woodward, ed., *Mary Chesnut's Civil War* (New Haven, Conn.: Yale University Press, 1981), 60, 83, diary entries of May 17, June 28, 1861, quoting conversations with Davis. See also C. Vann Woodward and Elisabeth Muhlenfeld, eds., *The Private Mary Chesnut: The Unpublished Civil War Diaries* (New York: Oxford University Press, 1984), 69, 86.

11. Rembert W. Patrick, *Jefferson Davis and His Cabinet* (Baton Rouge: Louisiana State University Press, 1944), 107–8; Paul Escott, *After Secession: Jefferson Davis and the Failure of Confederate Nationalism* (Baton Rouge: Louisiana State University Press, 1978), 115; John H. Reagan, *Memoirs, with Special Reference to Secession and the Civil War* (reprint of 1906 ed., Austin, Tex.: Pemberton Press, 1968), 116–17.

12. Rowland, *JDC,* 5:84.

13. Davis to Claiborne Fox Jackson, Apr. 23, 1861, ibid., 5:66.

14. Davis's message to Congress, ibid., 5:70–72.

15. W. C. Davis, *Davis,* 176; Cooper, *Davis,* 302, 315.

16. Davis to Robert Barnwell Rhett, Nov. 10, 1860, Crist, *PJD,* 6:369.

17. Davis to Edmund Kirby Smith, Nov. 19, 1863, ibid., 10:81.

18. Spencer Adams to Davis, May 1, 1861, Jacob Thompson to

Davis, Sept. 6, 1861, Corpus Christi Committee of Public Safety to Davis, Apr. 28, 1861, ibid., 7:143, 329, 141.

19. Charles J. Mitchell to Davis, Apr. 27, 1861, Thomas O. Moore to Davis, Apr. 28, Sept. 7, 1861, ibid., 7:134–35, 141, 331; Joseph E. Brown to J. H. Howard, May 20, 1861, in Joseph Howard Parks, *Joseph E. Brown of Georgia* (Baton Rouge: Louisiana State University Press, 1977), 147; Brown to Leroy P. Walker, May [?], 1861, in William Harris Bragg, *Joe Brown's Army: The Georgia State Line, 1862–1865* (Macon, Ga.: Mercer University Press, 1987), 4.

20. Davis to Isham G. Harris, July 17, 1861, Crist, *PJD,* 7:248; italics added.

21. Davis to Johnston, Sept. 5, 8, 1861, Davis to John Letcher, Sept. 13, 1861, Rowland, *JDC,* 5:129, 131, 135–36.

22. Davis's endorsement on a letter from Herschel V. Johnson to Davis, Nov. 11, 1861, Crist, *PJD,* 7:409; Davis to Pickens, Nov. 11, 1861, ibid., Addenda, 11:598; Parks, *Joseph E. Brown,* 168.

23. P. G. T. Beauregard to Davis, June 12, 1861, Davis to Beauregard, June 13, 1861, Crist, *PJD,* 7:197, 199–200.

24. Davis to James Chesnut, Oct. 30, 1861, Rowland, *JDC,* 5:157; Chesnut to Davis, Nov. 2, 1861, Robert E. Lee to Davis, Nov. 24, 1861, Crist, *PJD,* 7:388–92, 426.

25. Davis to Joseph Davis, June 18, 1861, Davis to Johnston, June 22, July 13, 1861, Crist, *PJD,* 7:203, 208–9, 239.

26. Rowland, *JDC,* 5:111; Crist, *PJD,* 7:249; *O.R.,* ser. 1, vol. 2:932, 980.

27. Steven E. Woodworth, *Davis and Lee at War* (Lawrence: University Press of Kansas, 1995), 6–7.

28. Leonidas Polk to Mrs. Polk, June 10, 1861, in W. C. Davis, *Davis,* 346; Johnston to Davis, June 26, 1861, Crist, *PJD,* 7:213.

29. W. C. Davis, *Davis,* 350–51; Cooper, *Davis,* 348; Woodworth, *Davis and Lee at War,* 1–5; Jefferson Davis, *The Rise and Fall of the Confederate Government,* 2 vols. (reprint of 1881 ed., New York: Da Capo Press, 1990), 1:302–5.

30. Crist, *PJD,* 7:258–59.

31. Woodworth, *Davis and Lee at War,* 43–44; Williams, *Beauregard,* 89–90.

32. Johnston to Davis, Aug. 3, 1861, Crist, *PJD,* 7:273.

33. Woodward and Muhlenfeld, *The Private Mary Chesnut,* 103, diary entry of July 24, 1861.

34. Quoted in Woodworth, *Davis and Lee at War,* 49.

35. Judah P. Benjamin to Beauregard, Oct. 17, 1861, Beauregard to Davis, Nov. 5, 1861, Davis to Beauregard, Nov. 10, 1861, *O.R.,* ser. 1, vol. 5:904, 945.

36. Davis to Beauregard, Oct. 30, 1861, Rowland, *JDC,* 5:156–57.

37. John B. Jones, *A Rebel War Clerk's Diary at the Confederate States Capital,* ed. Howard Swiggett, 2 vols. (New York: Old Hickory Bookshop, 1935), 1:71, entry of Aug. 11, 1861; Davis, *Rise and Fall,* 1:315–16.

38. Johnston to Davis, Sept. 12, 1861, *O.R.,* ser. 4, vol. 1:605–8.

39. Davis to Johnston, Sept. 14, 1861, Crist, *PJD,* 7:340.

40. *Richmond Examiner,* Sept. 27, 1861, in Frederick S. Daniel, *The Richmond Examiner During the War* (reprint ed. of 1868, New York: Arno Press, 1970), 23–24.

41. Wilmot D. De Saussure to James Chesnut, Oct. 4, 1861, in Woodward, *Mary Chesnut's Civil War,* 215.

42. Davis to William Brooks, Mar. 14, 1862, Crist, *PJD,* 8:100.

43. The main source for the discussions at this conference is Smith's memorandum, written in January 1862: *O.R.,* ser. 1, vol. 5:884–87.

See also Davis to Johnston, Sept. 8, Nov. 10, 1861, Rowland, *JDC*, 5:129, 161–63; Gustavus W. Smith to Davis, Oct. 8, 1861, Crist, *PJD*, 7:355; Davis to Smith, Oct. 10, 1861, Rowland, *JDC*, 5:139; Woodworth, *Davis and Lee at War*, 60–69.

2. WINTER OF DISCONTENT

1. Isham Harris to Jefferson Davis, Sept. 4, 1861, and Davis's endorsement, Leonidas Polk to Davis, Sept. 4, 1861, Davis to Polk, Sept. 5, 1861, Harris to Davis, Sept. 13, 1861, Davis to Polk, Sept. 15, 1861, Crist, *PJD*, 7:325–28 and n, 339, 341; Steven E. Woodworth, *Jefferson Davis and His Generals* (Lawrence: University Press of Kansas, 1990), 36–41; Steven E. Woodworth, *No Band of Brothers: Problems of the Rebel High Command* (Columbia: University of Missouri Press, 1999), 15–17; William J. Cooper, *Jefferson Davis, American* (New York: Alfred A. Knopf, 2000), 356–57; Herman Hattaway and Richard E. Beringer, *Jefferson Davis: Confederate President* (Lawrence: University Press of Kansas, 2002), 104–6.

2. Charles P. Roland, *Albert Sidney Johnston: Soldier of Three Republics* (Austin: University of Texas Press, 1964), 277. See also William C. Davis, *Jefferson Davis: The Man and His Hour* (New York: HarperCollins, 1991), 396–97.

3. *O.R.*, ser. 1, vol. 6:823–24.

4. Jefferson Davis to Joseph Davis, Feb. 21, 1862, Crist, *PJD*, 8:53.

5. Grady McWhiney, "Jefferson Davis and His Generals," in McWhiney, *Southerners and Other Americans* (New York: Basic Books, 1973), 90–91.

6. Roland, *Johnston*, 299–300.

7. Davis to Albert Sidney Johnston, Mar. 12, 1862, Crist, *PJD,* 8:92–94; Thomas Bragg diary, entry of Mar. 7, 1862, quoted in ibid., 8:94n.

8. Sidney Johnston to Davis, Mar. 18, 1862, *O.R.,* ser. 1, vol. 7:258–61; Davis to Johnston, Mar. 26, 1862, Crist, *PJD,* 8:117.

9. Davis to Judah P. Benjamin, Mar. 11, 1862, Rowland, *JDC,* 5:214.

10. *Richmond Whig,* Mar. 18, 1862, in Harrison Anthony Trexler, "The Davis Administration and the Richmond Press, 1861–1865," *Journal of Southern History* 16 (1950): 187; Toombs quoted in Cooper, *Davis,* 382.

11. Eli N. Evans, *Judah P. Benjamin: The Jewish Confederate* (New York: Free Press, 1988), 146–47; Cooper, *Davis,* 382–83; Rembert W. Patrick, *Jefferson Davis and His Cabinet* (Baton Rouge: Louisiana State University Press, 1944), 64–65, 173.

12. Rowland, *JDC,* 5:198–203.

13. Davis to William M. Brooks, Mar. 15, 1862, Crist, *PJD,* 8:100; Thomas Bragg diary, entry of Feb. 19, 1862, in Grady McWhiney, *Braxton Bragg and Confederate Defeat* (New York: Columbia University Press, 1969), 200.

14. Rowland, *JDC,* 5:203–4.

15. Sidney Johnston to Davis, Mar. 18, 1862, Davis to Johnston, Mar. 26, Apr. 5, 1862, Crist, *PJD,* 8:106, 117, 130.

16. P. G. T. Beauregard's telegram and Davis's message to Congress, ibid., 8:131, 138.

17. Cooper, *Davis,* 379; W. C. Davis, *Davis,* 404.

18. Davis to governors, Apr. 10, 1862, Rowland, *JDC,* 5:230; Joseph E. Brown to Davis, Apr. 10, 1862, Crist, *PJD,* 8:139; Davis to Brown, Apr. 11, 1862, Rowland, *JDC,* 5:230.

19. Beauregard to Samuel Cooper, May 19, 1862, *O.R.*, ser. 1, vol. 10, pt. 2:529–30.

20. Beauregard to Cooper, June 12, 1862, Crist, *PJD*, 8:245n; Davis to Varina Davis, June 13, 1862, ibid., 8:243–44.

21. Davis to William Preston Johnston, June 14, 1862, Rowland, *JDC*, 5:279–80.

22. Davis to Bragg, copy to Beauregard, June 20, 1862, ibid., 283. See also Crist, *PJD*, 8:254, and T. Harry Williams, *P. G. T. Beauregard: Napoleon in Gray* (Baton Rouge: Louisiana State University Press, 1955), 156–58.

23. Beauregard to Thomas Jordan, July 12, 1862, in Williams, *Beauregard,* 161.

24. Crist, *PJD*, 8:119–20; Archer Jones, *Confederate Strategy from Shiloh to Vicksburg* (Baton Rouge: Louisiana State University Press, 1961), 46–49; George Green Shackelford, *George Wythe Randolph and the Confederate Elite* (Athens: University of Georgia Press, 1988), 120–21; Frank E. Vandiver, *Their Tattered Flags: The Epic of the Confederacy* (New York: Harper's Magazine Press, 1970), 131.

25. Brown to Davis, May 8, June 21, 1862, *O.R.*, ser. 4, vol. 1:1116–20, 1156–69.

26. Davis to Brown, May 29, July 10, 1862, Rowland, *JDC*, 5:254–62, 292–93.

27. Davis's inaugural address, ibid., 5:199.

28. James M. Mathews, ed., *Public Laws of the Confederate States of America* (Richmond, Va., 1862), 1.

29. Mark E. Neely, *Southern Rights: Political Prisoners and the Myth of Confederate Constitutionalism* (Charlottesville: University Press of Virginia, 1999), 167.

30. Davis to Joseph E. Johnston, Feb. 19, 1862, Rowland, *JDC*, 5:197.

31. Steven E. Woodworth, *Davis and Lee at War* (Lawrence: University Press of Kansas, 1995), 94–105; Craig L. Symonds, *Joseph E. Johnston: A Civil War Biography* (New York: W. W. Norton, 1992), 136–38; letters and telegrams in Crist, *PJD*, 8:56, 67–68, 76, 81–82; Davis to Joseph Johnston, Mar. 10, 15, 1862, Rowland, *JDC*, 5:214, 222.

32. Davis to Robert E. Lee, Mar. 2, 1862, Lee to Davis, Mar. 2, 1862, Crist, *PJD*, 8:75, 76.

33. Ibid., 8:99; Cooper, *Davis*, 379–80; Paul D. Escott, *Military Necessity: Civil-Military Relations in the Confederacy* (Westport, Conn.: Praeger, 2006), 61.

34. Woodworth, *Davis and Lee at War*, 112–17; Joseph Harsh, *Confederate Tide Rising: Robert E. Lee and the Making of Southern Strategy, 1861–1862* (Kent, Ohio: Kent State University Press, 1998), 36–37; Symonds, *Johnston*, 141–42.

35. Davis to Joseph Johnston, May 1, 11, 1862, Rowland, *JDC*, 5:239–40; Crist, *PJD*, 8:170–71.

36. William K. Scarborough, ed., *The Diary of Edmund Ruffin*, 3 vols. (Baton Rouge: Louisiana State University Press, 1972–89), 2:308, entry of May 19, 1862; Helen Keary to her mother, May 7, 1862, in Edward A. Pollard, *Southern History of the War*, 2 vols. (New York: C. B. Richardson, 1866), 1:381–82.

37. Davis to Varina Davis, May 9, 1862, Crist, *PJD*, 8:168–69 and n; John B. Jones, *A Rebel War Clerk's Diary at the Confederate States Capital*, ed. Howard Swiggett, 2 vols. (New York: Old Hickory Bookshop, 1935), 1:126, entry of May 19, 1862.

38. Davis to Joseph Johnston, May 11, 1862, Johnston to his wife, May 12, 1862, Crist, *PJD*, 8:170–71 and 172n. See also Davis to Varina Davis, May 13, 1862, ibid., 8:174.

39. Letter headnote, ibid., 8:168; Cooper, *Davis,* 388.

40. *Richmond Examiner,* May 19, 1862, in Trexler, "The Davis Administration and the Richmond Press," 184.

41. Davis to Joseph Johnston, May 17, 1862, Crist, *PJD,* 8:184–85.

42. John H. Reagan, *Memoirs, with Special Reference to Secession and the Civil War* (reprint of 1906 ed., Austin, Tex.: Pemberton Press, 1968), 138–39; Woodworth, *Davis and Lee at War,* 133–34.

43. Davis to Varina Davis, May 19, 1862, Rowland, *JDC,* 5:248.

44. Reagan, *Memoirs,* 139.

45. Jones, *Rebel War Clerk's Diary,* 1:127, entry of May 20, 1862.

46. Davis to Johnston, May 23, 1862, *O.R.,* ser. 1, vol. 11, pt. 3:536; Davis to Varina Davis, May 28, 1862, Rowland, *JDC,* 5:252–54.

47. Davis to Varina Davis, May 30, 1862, Crist, *PJD,* 8:203.

48. Johnston to Louis T. Wigfall, Nov. 12, 1863, in Symonds, *Johnston,* 154.

49. *Memphis [Grenada] Appeal,* June 9, 1862, in Crist, *PJD,* 8:208.

50. Davis to Lee, June 1, 1862, Davis to Varina Davis, June 2, 1862, ibid., 207, 209.

3. War So Gigantic

1. *Richmond Dispatch,* May 6, 1862, *Charleston Mercury,* May 8, 1862, quoted in Richard Slotkin, *The Long Road to Antietam* (New York: W. W. Norton, 2012), 65.

2. Joseph Brown to Jefferson Davis, May 3, 1862, Crist, *PJD,* 8:162; Davis to Brown, May 5, 1862, Rowland, *JDC,* 5:241–42.

3. Robert E. Lee to Davis, June 5, 10, 1862, Crist, *PJD,* 8:225–26, 235; Steven E. Woodworth, *Davis and Lee at War* (Lawrence:

University Press of Kansas, 1995), 154; Joseph Harsh, *Confederate Tide Rising: Robert E. Lee and the Making of Southern Strategy, 1861–1862* (Kent, Ohio: Kent State University Press, 1998), 54.

4. Davis to Varina Davis, June 11, 1862, Crist, *PJD,* 8:235–36.

5. Slightly different versions of this incident were told by Burton Harrison, Davis's private secretary, and by James Chesnut, both of whom were present. Constance Cary Harrison, *Recollections Grave and Gay* (New York: Charles Scribner's Sons, 1911), 72–73; C. Vann Woodward, ed., *Mary Chesnut's Civil War* (New Haven, Conn.: Yale University Press, 1981), 410–11, diary entry of July 10, 1862.

6. James I. Robertson, *General A. P. Hill: The Story of a Confederate Warrior* (New York: Random House, 1987), 88.

7. Crist, *PJD,* 8:275–76.

8. Davis to John Forsyth, July 18, 1862, ibid., 8:293–95; Davis to Col. J. Foster Marshall, July 11, 1862, Rowland, *JDC,* 5:293.

9. Davis to Edmund Kirby Smith, July 28, 1862, Crist, *PJD,* 8:305.

10. Davis to Lee, Aug. 26, 1862, Rowland, *JDC,* 5:330. See also Harsh, *Confederate Tide Rising,* 143–44.

11. Lee to Davis, Sept. 3, 1862, Crist, *PJD,* 8:373–74.

12. Lee to Davis, Sept. 8, 1862, in Clifford Dowdey and Louis H. Manarin, eds., *The Wartime Papers of R. E. Lee* (New York: Bramhall House, 1961), 301.

13. William C. Davis, *Jefferson Davis: The Man and His Hour* (New York: HarperCollins, 1991), 468–69; Crist, *PJD,* 8:379–89; Davis to Lee, Sept. 28, 1862, Crist, *PJD,* 8:409.

14. Braxton Bragg to Davis, July 21, 22, Crist, *PJD,* 8:298, 299.

15. Davis to Edmund Kirby Smith, June 25, 1862, Rowland, *JDC,* 5:286.

16. Davis to Kirby Smith, July 28, 1862, Davis to Bragg, Aug. 5, 1862, Crist, *PJD*, 8:305, 322.

17. *O.R.*, ser. 1, vol. 19, pt. 2:596, 601–2.

18. Rowland, *JDC*, 5:338–39. Rowland dates this document Sept. 19, 1862, but Crist, *PJD*, 8:366, more convincingly dates it Sept. 12.

19. Bragg to Davis, Oct. 2, 1862, Crist, *PJD*, 8:417. See also ibid., 8:419n.

20. Davis to Theophilus Holmes, Oct. 21, 1862, ibid., 8:454–55; Robert Garlick Hill Kean, *Inside the Confederate Government: The Diary of Robert Garlick Hill Kean,* ed. Edward Younger (New York: Oxford University Press, 1957), 28, 86, entries of Oct. 19, 1862, July 27, 1863.

21. Davis to Zebulon Vance, Oct. 17, 1862, Frontis W. Johnston and Joe A. Mobley, eds., *The Papers of Zebulon Baird Vance,* 2 vols. (Raleigh: North Carolina Department of Cultural Resources, 1963–95), 1:268–69; Davis to John C. Pemberton, June 4, 1862, Rowland, *JDC,* 5:267.

22. John Milton to Davis, Oct. 10, 1862, Crist, *PJD,* 8:438; Davis to John G. Shorter, Oct. 28, 1862, Rowland, *JDC,* 5:361.

23. Thomas O. Moore to Davis, June 2, 1862, Crist, *PJD*, 8:212–15. See also Davis to Lucien J. Dupree, Oct. 11, 1862, and Thomas O. Moore to Davis, Dec. 1, 1862, ibid., 8:352–53, 525.

24. Proclamation of Arkansas governor, ibid., 8:194n.

25. Robert L. Kerby, *Kirby Smith's Confederacy: The Trans-Mississippi South, 1863–1865* (New York: Columbia University Press, 1972), 31–32; Daniel E. Sutherland, *A Savage Conflict: The Decisive Role of Guerrillas in the American Civil War* (Chapel Hill: University of North Carolina Press, 2009), 66–67; Mark E. Neely, *Southern*

Rights: Political Prisoners and the Myth of Confederate Constitution-alism (Charlottesville: University Press of Virginia, 1999), 24–25; Davis to Earl Van Dorn, May 20, 1862, Crist, *PJD,* 8:193–94; Davis's endorsement on a letter from Thomas Moore, July 10, 1862, Crist, *PJD,* 8:287; Davis to Francis R. Lubbock, Aug. 15, 1862, Rowland, *JDC,* 5:318.

26. Davis to Holmes, Dec. 21, 1862, Crist, *PJD,* 8:561–62.

27. Holmes to Davis, Dec. 29, 1862, ibid., 8:585; Harris Flanagin to Davis, Jan. 5, 1863, ibid., 9:10.

28. Davis to Holmes, Jan. 28, 1863, ibid., 8:587n.

29. *Diary of Robert G. H. Kean,* 100, entry of Aug. 23, 1863; John B. Jones, *A Rebel War Clerk's Diary at the Confederate States Capital,* ed. Howard Swiggett, 2 vols. (New York: Old Hickory Bookshop, 1935), 1:204, 44, entries of Dec. 4, 1862, May 26, 1861.

30. Stephen Mallory's diary, entry of Sept. 19, 1862, Mallory to his son "Buddy," Sept. 27, 1865, in Joseph T. Durkin, *Stephen R. Mallory: Confederate Navy Chief* (Chapel Hill: University of North Carolina Press, 1954), 249, 176.

31. Jones, *Rebel War Clerk's Diary,* 1:190, entry of Nov. 15, 1862; *Diary of Robert G. H. Kean,* 30–31, entry of Nov. 25, 1862.

32. George Green Shackelford, *George Wythe Randolph and the Confederate Elite* (Athens: University of Georgia Press, 1988), 44–45.

33. Davis to George W. Randolph, Nov. 12, 14, 1862, Rowland, *JDC,* 5:369, 371–72; Randolph to Davis, Nov. 15, 1862, Davis to Randolph, Nov. 15, 1862, Crist, *PJD,* 8:495–96.

34. Jones, *Rebel War Clerk's Diary,* 1:190, entry of Nov. 17, 1862.

35. *Diary of Robert G. H. Kean,* 153, entry of May 30, 1864.

36. Davis to Bragg, Aug. 5, 1862, Crist, *PJD*, 8:321–22.

37. Davis to Edmund Kirby Smith, Oct. 29, 1862, ibid, 8:468–70.

38. William J. Cooper, *Jefferson Davis, American* (New York: Alfred A. Knopf, 2000), 412–14; W. C. Davis, *Davis*, 475–76; Craig L. Symonds, *Joseph E. Johnston: A Civil War Biography* (New York: W. W. Norton, 1992), 173–80.

39. W. C. Davis, *Davis*, 481–84; Cooper, *Davis*, 415–17; Archer Jones, *Confederate Strategy from Shiloh to Vicksburg* (Baton Rouge: Louisiana State University Press, 1961), 117–18, 125.

40. Davis to Lee, Dec. 8, 1862, Crist, *PJD*, 8:553.

41. Rowland, *JDC*, 5:114; Crist, *PJD*, 7:416–17.

42. Paul D. Escott, *After Secession: Jefferson Davis and the Failure of Confederate Nationalism* (Baton Rouge: Louisiana State University Press, 1978), 179–80.

43. Crist, *PJD*, 8:566–67, 9:11–13.

44. *O.R.*, ser. 1, vol. 15:906–8.

45. Rowland, *JDC*, 5:408–11.

46. General H. W. Mercer to General Thomas Jordan, Nov. 14, 1862, James Seddon to General P. G. T. Beauregard, Nov. 30, 1862, *O. R.*, ser. 2, vol. 4:945–46, 954.

47. Crist, *PJD*, 8:575.

4. THE CLOUDS ARE DARK OVER US

1. *O.R.*, ser. 1, vol. 20, pt. 1:662; vol. 52, pt. 1:402.

2. Jefferson Davis to Joseph E. Johnston, Jan. 21, 1863, Crist, *PJD*, 9:35; Davis to Johnston, Jan. 22, 1863, Rowland, *JDC*, 5:420–21.

3. Leonidas Polk to Davis, Feb. 4, 1863, Bragg to Davis, Jan. 17, 1863, Crist, *PJD,* 9:50–51, 28.

4. Johnston to Louis T. Wigfall, Jan. 26, 1863, in Louise Wigfall, *A Southern Girl in '61: The Wartime Memories of a Confederate Senator's Daughter* (New York: Doubleday, Page, 1905), 122–23.

5. Johnston to Davis, Feb. 3, 12, 1863, Crist, *PJD,* 9:48–49, 59–60.

6. Davis to Johnston, Feb. 19, 1863, ibid., 9:66–67.

7. *O.R.,* ser. 1, vol. 23, pt. 2:674; William J. Cooper, *Jefferson Davis, American* (New York: Alfred A. Knopf, 2000), 423.

8. Johnston to Davis, Apr. 10, 1863, Crist, *PJD,* 9:137.

9. Davis to Robert E. Lee, May 4, 1863, Davis to Joseph Davis, May 7, 1863, ibid., 9:165, 167.

10. Davis to Johnston, Jan. 7, 1863, Davis to Joseph Davis, May 7, 1863, ibid., 9:17, 166.

11. James Longstreet, *From Manassas to Appomattox* (Philadelphia: Lippincott, 1895), 218; Lee to James Seddon, May 10, 1863, Crist, *PJD,* 9:179.

12. Steven E. Woodworth, *Davis and Lee at War* (Lawrence: University Press of Kansas, 1995), 227–33; John B. Jones, *A Rebel War Clerk's Diary at the Confederate States Capital,* ed. Howard Swiggett, 2 vols. (New York: Old Hickory Bookshop, 1935), 1:325–26, entries of May 15 and 16, 1863; John H. Reagan, *Memoirs, with Special Reference to Secession and the Civil War* (reprint of 1906 ed., Austin, Tex.: Pemberton Press, 1968), 121–22, 150–51.

13. Sarah Woolfolk Wiggins, ed., *The Journals of Josiah Gorgas, 1857–1878* (Tuscaloosa: University of Alabama Press, 1995), 57, entry of Mar. 23, 1863.

14. James Seddon to Johnston, May 9, 1863, *O.R.*, ser. 1, vol. 23, pt. 2:825–26; Johnston to Seddon, May 13, 16, ibid., vol. 24, pt. 1:215–16.

15. Davis to John C. Pemberton, May 7, 1863, Rowland, *JDC,* 5:482; Steven E. Woodworth, *Jefferson Davis and His Generals* (Lawrence: University Press of Kansas, 1990), 206–7; James R. Arnold, *Presidents Under Fire: Commanders in Chief in Victory and Defeat* (New York: Orion Books, 1994), 170.

16. Rowland, *JDC,* 5:489–90; Crist, *PJD,* 9:186–200, 202–3, 215–19, 239–40.

17. Craig L. Symonds, *Joseph E. Johnston: A Civil War Biography* (New York: W. W. Norton, 1992), 201; Michael B. Ballard, *Pemberton: A Biography* (Jackson: University Press of Mississippi, 1991), 177.

18. Quotations in Samuel Carter, *The Final Fortress: The Campaign for Vicksburg 1862–1863* (New York: St. Martin's Press, 1980), 207, and Peter F. Walker, *Vicksburg: A People at War* (Chapel Hill: University of North Carolina Press, 1960), 187–88.

19. Johnston to Seddon, June 15, 1863, Seddon to Johnston, June 16, 1863, *O.R.,* ser. 1, vol. 24, pt. 1:227; Robert Garlick Hill Kean, *Inside the Confederate Government: The Diary of Robert Garlick Hill Kean*, ed. Edward Younger (New York: Oxford University Press, 1957), entry of June 14, 1863.

20. Wiggins, *Journals of Gorgas,* 74, entry of July 17, 1863.

21. Davis to Johnston, July 8, 11, 1863, Crist, *PJD,* 9:264, 271; Richard M. McMurry, "'The Enemy at Richmond': Joseph E. Johnston and the Confederate Government," in John T. Hubbell, ed., *Conflict and Command* (Kent, Ohio: Kent State University Press, 2012), 198.

22. Davis to Robert W. Johnson, July 14, 1863, Crist, *PJD,* 9:276; Davis to Theophilus Holmes, July 15, 1863, Rowland, *JDC,* 5:555.

23. Davis to Johnston, July 15, 1863, Rowland, *JDC,* 5:556–63; Johnston to Davis, Aug. 8, 1863, *O.R.,* ser. 1, vol. 24, pt. 1:209–13; Symonds, *Johnston,* 209–11.

24. Symonds, *Johnston,* 212–14, quotation on p. 212.

25. *Brandon Republican,* Oct. 29, 1863, reprinted in *Richmond Whig,* Nov. 9, 1863, in Crist, *PJD,* 9:335n.

26. Ethelbert Barksdale to Davis, July 29, 1863, Rowland, *JDC,* 5:581–82; James Phelan to Davis, Aug. 14, 1863, Crist, *PJD,* 9:343.

27. *Richmond Examiner,* Aug. 5, 1863, in Frederick S. Daniel, *The Richmond Examiner During the War* (reprint of 1868 ed., New York: Arno Press, 1970), 107–9.

28. C. Vann Woodward, ed., *Mary Chesnut's Civil War* (New Haven, Conn.: Yale University Press, 1981), 482–83, entry of October 1863 (no day).

29. *Richmond Examiner,* July 7, 1863. The Battle of Gettysburg had been over for three days when this editorial appeared, but the news took several days to reach Richmond.

30. Clifford Dowdey and Louis H. Manarin, eds., *The Wartime Papers of R. E. Lee* (New York: Bramhall House, 1961), 507–9.

31. Alexander H. Stephens to Davis, June 12, 1863, Davis to Stephens, July 2, 1863, Rowland, *JDC,* 5:513–16; Davis to Stephens, June 18, 1863, Crist, *PJD,* 9:229.

32. Thomas E. Schott, "The Stephens 'Peace' Mission," *North and South* 1 (Oct. 1998): 39–40.

33. Davis to Lee, June 28, 1863, Crist, *PJD,* 9:247–49. See also Lee to Davis, May 7, June 7, 23, 1863, Davis to Lee, May 9, 31, 1863,

ibid., 9:170, 198, 202, 209, 236–37; and Woodworth, *Davis and Lee at War,* 234–39.

34. Lincoln to Samuel Phillips Lee, July 4, 1863, in Roy P. Basler, ed., *The Collected Works of Abraham Lincoln,* 9 vols. (New Brunswick, N.J.: Rutgers University Press, 1953–55), 6:317.

35. Davis to Lee, July 28, 1863, Wigfall to Clement C. Clay, Aug. 13, 1863, Crist, *PJD,* 9:308, 311n.

36. Lee to Davis, Aug. 8, 1863, Davis to Lee, Aug. 11, 1863, ibid., 326–27, 337–38.

37. B. T. Kavanaugh to Davis, Aug. 13, 1863, Davis to Holmes, Nov. 19, 1863, Rowland, *JDC,* 5:590–92, 6:84–85.

38. Davis to Edmund Kirby Smith, Apr. 28, 1864, ibid., 6:237. See also Davis to Smith, July 14, 1863, Crist, *PJD,* 9:279.

39. Robert L. Kerby, *Kirby Smith's Confederacy: The Trans-Mississippi South, 1863–1865* (New York: Columbia University Press, 1972).

40. Woodworth, *Davis and His Generals,* 226–28.

41. Davis to Lee, Aug. 24, Sept. 8, 1863, Lee to Davis, Sept. 6, 14, 1863, Crist, *PJD,* 9:353, 373, 375, 385–86, 387n; Woodworth, *Davis and Lee at War,* 255–57; Cooper, *Davis,* 453–54.

42. Woodworth, *Davis and His Generals,* 230–33.

43. Jones, *Rebel War Clerk's Diary,* 2:50, entry of Sept. 22, 1863.

44. Polk to Davis, Sept. 27, 1863, Crist, *PJD,* 9:410.

45. Braxton Bragg to Davis, Sept. 25, 1863, ibid., 9:404–6; Davis to Bragg, Sept. 30, 1863, Rowland, *JDC,* 6:53; Davis to Bragg, Oct. 3, 1863, Crist, *PJD,* 10:6.

46. Dated Oct. 4, 1863, in Crist, *PJD,* 10:9.

47. Ibid., 10:40–41n; Woodworth, *Davis and His Generals,* 238–44.

48. Bragg to Davis, Oct. 11, 1863, Davis to Bragg, Oct. 13, 29, 1863,

Howell Cobb to Davis, Nov. 6, 1863, Crist, *PJD,* 10:23–24, 36–37, 54–55.

49. Davis to Bragg, Oct. 29, 1863, ibid., 10:37–38.

50. Crist, *PJD,* 10:35–54.

51. Jones, *Rebel War Clerk's Diary,* 2:88, entry of Nov. 3, 1863.

52. Bragg to Davis, Dec. 1, 1863, Crist, *PJD,* 10:94–95 and n; *O.R.,* ser. 1, vol. 31, pt. 2:682.

53. William K. Scarborough, ed., *The Diary of Edmund Ruffin,* 3 vols. (Baton Rouge: Louisiana State University Press, 1972–89), 3:250–51, entry of Dec. 2, 1863; Beth G. Crabtree and James W. Patton, eds., *"Journal of a Secesh Lady": The Diary of Catherine Ann Devereux Edmondston, 1860–1866* (Raleigh: North Carolina Division of Archives and History, 1979), 505–6, entry of Dec. 11, 1863.

54. Lee to Davis, Dec. 3, 1863, Davis to Lee, Dec. 6, 1863, Lee to Davis, Dec. 7, 1863 (telegram and letter), Davis to Lee, Dec. 8, 1863, Davis to Johnston, Dec. 16, 23, 1863, Crist, *PJD,* 10:99, 101, 102, 104, 105–6, 112, 119–21; Steven E. Woodworth, *No Band of Brothers: Problems of the Rebel High Command* (Columbia: University of Missouri Press, 1999), 81–86; Symonds, *Johnston,* 222.

5. We Should Take the Initiative

1. Sarah Woolfolk Wiggins, ed., *The Journals of Josiah Gorgas, 1857–1878* (Tuscaloosa: University of Alabama Press, 1995), 98.

2. Frontis W. Johnston and Joe A. Mobley, eds., *The Papers of Zebulon Baird Vance,* 2 vols. (Raleigh: North Carolina Department of Cultural Resources, 1963–95), 1:279n.

3. C. Vann Woodward, ed., *Mary Chesnut's Civil War* (New Haven, Conn.: Yale University Press, 1981), 438, diary entry of Sept. 23, 1863.

4. Paul D. Escott, *Military Necessity: Civil-Military Relations in the Confederacy* (Westport, Conn.: Praeger, 2006), 47; Jeremy P. Felt, "Lucius B. Northrop and the Confederacy's Subsistence Department," *Virginia Magazine of History and Biography* 69 (1961): 181–93; John B. Jones, *A Rebel War Clerk's Diary at the Confederate States Capital,* ed. Howard Swiggett, 2 vols. (New York: Old Hickory Bookshop, 1935), 2:131, 136, entries of Jan. 18, 19, 26, 1864.

5. George W. Randolph to Jefferson Davis, Oct. 30, 1862, Davis's endorsement on a letter from Charles Jones, Nov. 14, 1862, in Crist, *PJD,* 8:473–74, 492.

6. Charles Jones to Davis, Nov. 10, 14, 1862, ibid., 8:486, 492; Jones, *Rebel War Clerk's Diary,* 1:179–80, 183, 185, 198, entries of Nov. 1, 6, 8, 28, 1862; Robert Garlick Hill Kean, *Inside the Confederate Government: The Diary of Robert Garlick Hill Kean,* ed. Edward Younger (New York: Oxford University Press, 1957), 32, entry of Nov. 30, 1862.

7. Davis to Edmund Kirby Smith, July 14, 1863, Rowland, *JDC,* 5:554; Robert L. Kerby, *Kirby Smith's Confederacy: The Trans-Mississippi South, 1863–1865* (New York: Columbia University Press, 1972), 156, 160; Ludwell H. Johnson, "Trading with the Union: The Evolution of Confederate Policy," *Virginia Magazine of History and Biography* 78 (1970): 316, 320.

8. Emory M. Thomas, *The Confederate Nation, 1861–1865* (New York: Harper & Row, 1979), 201–6; Stephanie McCurry, *Confederate Reckoning: Power and Politics in the Civil War South* (Cambridge, Mass.: Harvard University Press, 2010), 178–207; Emory

Thomas, *The Confederate State of Richmond: A Biography of the Capital* (Austin: University of Texas Press, 1971), 117–22; Ernest B. Furgurson, *Ashes of Glory: Richmond at War* (New York: Alfred A. Knopf, 1996), 193–96; William C. Davis, *Jefferson Davis: The Man and His Hour* (New York: HarperCollins, 1991), 497–98.

9. W. C. Davis, *Davis*, 537–38; Woodward, *Mary Chesnut's Civil War*, 437–38, 499, 551 and n, diary entries of Sept. 23, Dec. 5, 1863, Jan. 31, 1864; Alvy L. King, *Louis T. Wigfall: Southern Fire-Eater* (Baton Rouge: Louisiana State University Press, 1970), 177–78; *Diary of Robert G. H. Kean*, 89–90, 126–27, 133, 136, diary entries of Aug. 9, Dec. 14, 1863, Jan. 28, Feb. 10, 1864; Davis to the Senate, Jan. 27, 1864, Crist, *PJD*, 10:206.

10. *O.R.*, ser. 2, vol. 5:940–41.

11. Ibid., 5:128, 696.

12. Davis to Leonidas Polk, Apr. 30, 1864, Crist, *PJD*, 10:375.

13. Roy P. Basler, ed., *The Collected Works of Abraham Lincoln*, 9 vols. (New Brunswick, N.J.: Rutgers University Press, 1953–55), 6:357.

14. Jefferson Davis, *The Rise and Fall of the Confederate Government*, 2 vols. (reprint of 1881 ed., New York: Da Capo Press, 1990), 2:507.

15. Davis to Zebulon Vance, July 24, 1863, Rowland, *JDC*, 5:576–77; Vance to Davis, July 26, 1863, Crist, *PJD*, 9:306.

16. Vance to William A. Graham, Jan. 1, 1864, in Richard E. Yates, *The Confederacy and Zeb Vance* (Tuscaloosa: University of Alabama Press, 1958), 95.

17. Vance to Davis, Dec. 30, 1863, Rowland, *JDC*, 6:141–42.

18. Davis to Vance, Jan. 8, 1864, Crist, *PJD*, 10:158–62.

19. Davis's message to Congress, Feb. 3, 1864, Rowland, *JDC*, 6:164–69.

20. Vance to Davis, Feb. 9, 1864, and Davis's endorsement on the letter, and Davis to Vance, Feb. 29, 1864, Crist, *PJD*, 10:227–28, 268.

21. W. Buck Yearns and John G. Barrett, eds., *North Carolina Civil War Documentary* (Chapel Hill: University of North Carolina Press, 1980), 302–4; Mark W. Kruman, *Parties and Politics in North Carolina, 1836–1865* (Baton Rouge: Louisiana State University Press, 1983), 249–65.

22. Herschel V. Johnson to Davis, Jan. 4, 1864, Johnson to Alexander Stephens, July 11, 1864, Crist, *PJD*, 10:152–53 and 153n.

23. Davis to Clement C. Clay and Jacob Thompson, Apr. 27, 1864, Crist, *PJD*, 10:68–69; Jacob Thompson to Judah P. Benjamin, Dec. 3, 1864, *O.R.*, ser. 1, vol. 43, pt. 2:930–36; Larry E. Nelson, *Bullets, Ballots, and Rhetoric: Confederate Policy for the United States Presidential Contest of 1864* (Tuscaloosa: University of Alabama Press, 1980), 21–24; Oscar A. Kinchen, *Confederate Operations in Canada and the North* (North Quincy, Mass.: Christopher Publishing House, 1970), passim.

24. William J. Hardee to J. C. Ives, Dec. 24, 1863, *O.R.*, ser. 1, vol. 31, pt. 3:860.

25. Davis to Joseph E. Johnston, Dec. 23, 1863, Crist, *PJD*, 10:119–21. See also James Seddon to Johnston, Dec. 18, 1863, ibid., 10:121n.

26. Johnston to Davis, Jan. 2, 1864, ibid., 10:144–46.

27. Johnston to Davis, Feb. 1, 1864, William M. Browne to Davis, Feb. 14, 1864, ibid., 10:215–16, 233–34; Richard M. McMurry, "'The Enemy at Richmond': Joseph E. Johnston and the Confederate Government," in John T. Hubbell, ed., *Conflict and Command* (Kent, Ohio: Kent State University Press, 2012), 213–14.

28. Polk to Davis, Feb. 9, 1864, Davis to Johnston, Feb. 11, 1864, Johnston to Davis, Feb. 13, 1864, Davis to Johnston, Feb. 15, 17, 1864, Davis to Hardee, Feb. 21, 1864, Davis to Polk, Feb. 23, 1864, Crist, *PJD*, 10:227, 232, 234–35, 256, 259, and Rowland, *JDC*, 6:170–72; interview of Davis with William D. Gale, July 30, 1864, Crist, *PJD*, 10:571.

29. Herman Hattaway and Richard E. Beringer, *Jefferson Davis, Confederate President* (Lawrence: University Press of Kansas, 2002), 319–21; Craig L. Symonds, *Joseph E. Johnston: A Civil War Biography* (New York: W. W. Norton, 1992), 236–38; Herman Hattaway, "The General Whom the President Elevated Too High," in Gabor S. Boritt, ed., *Jefferson Davis's Generals* (New York: Oxford University Press, 1999), 92–93.

30. John Bell Hood to Davis, Mar. 7, 1864, *O.R.*, ser. 1, vol. 32, pt. 3:606–7.

31. Davis to James Longstreet, Mar. 7, 1864, Rowland, *JDC*, 6:199–201.

32. Longstreet to Johnston, Mar. 14, 1864, Crist, *PJD*, 10:290, 293–94n; Symonds, *Johnston*, 234–36; Steven E. Woodworth, *Jefferson Davis and His Generals* (Lawrence: University Press of Kansas, 1990), 272–74.

33. Hood to Bragg, Apr. 13, 1864, in Richard M. McMurry, *John Bell Hood and the War for Southern Independence* (Lexington: University Press of Kentucky, 1982), 97.

34. *Richmond Examiner* quoted in Jones, *Rebel War Clerk's Diary*, 2:157, entry of Feb. 25, 1864; Beth G. Crabtree and James W. Patton, eds., *"Journal of a Secesh Lady": The Diary of Catherine Ann Devereux Edmondston, 1860–1866* (Raleigh: North Carolina Division of Archives and History, 1979), 531, entry of Feb. 28, 1864.

35. Woodward, *Mary Chesnut's Civil War*, 643, diary entry of Sept. 19, 1864; Crist, *PJD*, 10:252n.

6. WE MUST BEAT SHERMAN

1. Rowland, *JDC*, 6:247–48, 250.

2. Varina Howell Davis, *Jefferson Davis, Ex-President of the Confederate States of America: A Memoir by His Wife*, 2 vols. (New York: Belford, 1890), 498; Rowland, *JDC*, 6:253.

3. Crist, *PJD*, 10:423; John H. Reagan, *Memoirs, with Special Reference to Secession and the Civil War* (reprint of 1906 ed., Austin, Tex.: Pemberton Press, 1968), 191.

4. Crist, *PJD*, 10:423; Steven E. Woodworth, *No Band of Brothers: Problems of the Rebel High Command* (Columbia: University of Missouri Press, 1999), 106–8.

5. Jefferson Davis to Robert E. Lee, May 20, 1864, Crist, *PJD*, 10:424–26 and 427–28n; Woodworth, *No Band of Brothers*, 108–14.

6. Sarah Woolfolk Wiggins, ed., *The Journals of Josiah Gorgas, 1857–1878* (Tuscaloosa: University of Alabama Press, 1995), 108, diary entry of May 20, 1864.

7. Robert Ransom and Burton Harrison quoted in Crist, *PJD*, 10:459n.

8. John B. Jones, *A Rebel War Clerk's Diary at the Confederate States Capital*, ed. Howard Swiggett, 2 vols. (New York: Old Hickory Bookshop, 1935), 2:272, 275, entries of Aug. 25, 30, 1864.

9. Davis to Joseph E. Johnston, May 18, 1864, Davis to Lee, May 20, 1864, Crist, *PJD*, 10:420, 426. See also ibid., 10:432n.

10. Johnston to Davis, May 20, 21, 1864, ibid., 10:433, 434.

11. John Bell Hood to Davis, May 21, 1864, ibid., 10:434.

12. C. Vann Woodward, ed., *Mary Chesnut's Civil War* (New Haven, Conn.: Yale University Press, 1981), 616, 624, entries of June 4 and July 25, 1864; Robert Garlick Hill Kean, *Inside the Confederate Government: The Diary of Robert Garlick Hill Kean,* ed. Edward Younger (New York: Oxford University Press, 1957), 151, entry of May 22, 1864.

13. Davis's endorsement on a telegram from Maj. Gen. Stephen D. Lee to Braxton Bragg, June 22, 1864, Davis to Johnston, July 7, 11, 1864, Johnston to Davis, July 8, 12, 1864, Crist, *PJD,* 10:503, 508, 513–14, 516; Davis to Johnston (letter), July 11, 1864, Rowland, *JDC,* 6:289–91.

14. Steven E. Woodworth, *Jefferson Davis and His Generals* (Lawrence: University Press of Kansas, 1990), 278–79; Thomas Connelly and Archer Jones, *The Politics of Command: Factions and Ideas in Confederate Strategy* (Baton Rouge: Louisiana State University Press, 1973), 160; Craig L. Symonds, *Joseph E. Johnston: A Civil War Biography* (New York: W. W. Norton, 1992), 274–75, 281.

15. Joseph Brown to Davis, June 28, 1864, Davis to Brown, June 29, 1864, Crist, *PJD,* 10:492.

16. Brown to Davis, July 5, 1864, Davis to Brown, July 5, 1864, Brown to Davis, July 7, 1864, ibid., 10:501, 506.

17. Johnston to Davis, July 8, 1864, ibid., 10:508–9.

18. Davis to Bragg, July 9, 1864, Benjamin H. Hill to William T. Walthall, Oct. 12, 1878, recounting Hill's interview with Davis, ibid., 10:509, 513.

19. Davis to Lee, July 12, 1864, Lee to Davis, July 12, 1864, ibid., 10:513.

20. Lee to Davis, July 12, 1864, Davis to Lee, July 13, 1864, ibid., 517, 519.

21. Bragg to Davis, July 15, 1864 (telegram), Bragg to Davis, July 15, 1864 (letter), ibid., 10:522–25.

22. *Diary of Robert G. H. Kean,* 166, diary entry of July 14, 1864.

23. Crist, *PJD,* 10:531–32.

24. *O.R.,* ser. 1, vol. 38, pt. 5:885; Symonds, *Johnston,* 295.

25. Davis to Hood, Aug. 5, 1864, Crist, *PJD,* 10:586.

26. Johnson to Davis, Aug. 9, 1864, ibid., 10:599.

27. *New York World,* July 12, 1864.

28. James M. McPherson, *Tried by War: Abraham Lincoln as Commander in Chief* (New York: Penguin Press, 2008), 231–37.

29. No official record of this meeting was kept. This account and the quotations are taken from Gilmore's article in *Atlantic Monthly* 8 (Sept. 1864): 372–83. Gilmore wrote a briefer version describing the meeting in the *Boston Transcript,* July 22, 1864, and a longer one in his memoirs many years later. These versions vary slightly in detail but agree in substance, as does Judah Benjamin's account in a circular sent to Confederate envoys abroad after Gilmore's article was published in the *Atlantic Monthly.* Crist, *PJD,* 10:533–34, excerpts Gilmore's *Atlantic Monthly* article and Benjamin's circular.

30. Roy P. Basler, ed., *The Collected Works of Abraham Lincoln,* 9 vols. (New Brunswick, N.J.: Rutgers University Press, 1953–55), 8:151.

31. Edward McPherson, *The Political History of the United States*

During the Great Rebellion, 2nd ed. (Washington, D.C.: Government Printing Office, 1865), 419–20.

32. Allan Nevins and Milton Halsey Thomas, eds., *The Diary of George Templeton Strong,* 4 vols. (New York: Macmillan, 1952), 3:479, entry of Sept. 2, 1864; Alexander H. Stephens to Herschel V. Johnson, Sept. 5, 1864, and *Charleston Mercury* both quoted in Larry E. Nelson, *Bullets, Ballots, and Rhetoric: Confederate Policy for the United States Presidential Contest of 1864* (Tuscaloosa: University of Alabama Press, 1980), 115, 113. Neither Stephens nor the editor of the *Mercury* had learned of the fall of Atlanta when they penned these remarks.

33. *O.R.,* ser. 1, vol. 38, pt. 5:777.

34. *Richmond Examiner,* Sept. 5, 1864.

35. North Carolinian quoted in Nelson, *Bullets, Ballots, and Rhetoric,* 119; Woodward, *Mary Chesnut's Civil War,* 645, 648, diary entries of Sept. 21, 29, 1864.

36. *Richmond Examiner,* Sept. 5, 1864.

37. Davis speech at Macon, Georgia, Sept. 23, 1864, in Crist, *PJD,* 11:61.

38. Ibid., 61–63.

39. Horace Porter, *Campaigning with Grant* (New York: Century, 1897), 313.

40. Crist, *PJD,* 11:83.

41. Nelson, *Bullets, Ballots, and Rhetoric,* 131–32; Rowland, *JDC,* 6:358.

42. Crist, *PJD,* 11:91–92.

43. Ibid., 10:587n, 592, 11:35–36, 46–47, 67–68; Rowland, *JDC,* 6:344–45, 348; T. Harry Williams, *P. G. T. Beauregard: Na-*

poleon in Gray (Baton Rouge: Louisiana State University Press, 1955), 241–42.

44. Woodworth, *Davis and His Generals,* 292–94.

45. William T. Sherman to Ulysses S. Grant, Oct. 9, 11, 1864, *O.R.,* ser. 1, vol. 39, pt. 3:162, 202.

46. Rowland, *JDC,* 6:386.

7. The Last Resort

1. Jefferson Davis to John Bell Hood, Nov. 7, 1864, Crist, *PJD,* 11:145. See also William J. Cooper, *Jefferson Davis, American* (New York: Alfred A. Knopf, 2000), 499–500; Herman Hattaway and Richard E. Beringer, *Jefferson Davis, Confederate President* (Lawrence: University Press of Kansas, 2002), 340–41; and Steven E. Woodworth, *Jefferson Davis and His Generals* (Lawrence: University Press of Kansas, 1990), 294–95.

2. Jefferson Davis, *The Rise and Fall of the Confederate Government,* 2 vols. (reprint of 1881 ed., New York: Da Capo Press, 1990), 2:482–83; William J. Cooper, "A Reassessment of Jefferson Davis as War Leader: The Case from Atlanta to Nashville," *Journal of Southern History* 36 (1970): 199–204.

3. Davis to Howell Cobb, Nov. 18, 1864, Beauregard to Samuel Cooper, Nov. 18, 1864, with Davis's endorsement, Davis to Hardee, Nov. 24, 1864, Davis to Beauregard, Nov. 30, 1864, P. A. Lawson to Davis, Dec. 27, 1864, Davis to Hugh R. Davis, Jan. 8, 1865, Crist, *PJD,* 11:170, 171, 184, 194, 255, 287; Davis to William M. Browne, Nov. 22, 1864, Rowland, *JDC,* 6:410.

4. *Richmond Examiner,* Dec. 21, 1864, in Frederick S. Daniel, *The* Richmond Examiner *During the War* (reprint of 1868 ed., New York: Arno Press, 1970), 215; Louis T. Wigfall quoted in Crist, *PJD,* 11:264n.

5. Virginia Clay quoted in Michael B. Ballard, *A Long Shadow: Jefferson Davis and the Final Days of the Confederacy* (Jackson: University Press of Mississippi, 1986), 27; Sarah Woolfolk Wiggins, ed., *The Journals of Josiah Gorgas, 1857–1878* (Tuscaloosa: University of Alabama Press, 1995), 147–48, entry of Jan. 6, 1865.

6. John B. Jones, *A Rebel War Clerk's Diary at the Confederate States Capital,* ed. Howard Swiggett, 2 vols. (New York: Old Hickory Bookshop, 1935), 2:359, entry of Jan. 17, 1865; Beth G. Crabtree and James W. Patton, eds., *"Journal of a Secesh Lady": The Diary of Catherine Ann Devereux Edmondston, 1860–1866* (Raleigh: North Carolina Division of Archives and History, 1979), 658, entry of Jan. 22, 1865.

7. Robert Garlick Hill Kean, *Inside the Confederate Government: The Diary of Robert Garlick Hill Kean,* ed. Edward Younger (New York: Oxford University Press, 1957), 190, entry of Jan. 22, 1865.

8. Davis to James F. Johnson and Hugh W. Sheffey, Jan. 18, 1865, Crist, *PJD,* 11:335–37 and n; Steven E. Woodworth, *Davis and Lee at War* (Lawrence: University Press of Kansas, 1995), 309–11; Paul D. Escott, *Military Necessity: Civil-Military Relations in the Confederacy* (Westport, Conn.: Praeger, 2006), 155–57.

9. Richard Hawes to Davis, Jan. 11, 1865, Crist, *PJD,* 11:305–6.

10. Alexander H. Stephens and congressmen cited in ibid., 11:309n; Larry E. Nelson, *Bullets, Ballots, and Rhetoric: Confederate Policy for the United States Presidential Contest of 1864* (Tuscaloosa: University of Alabama Press, 1980), 164–65.

11. Francis Preston Blair to Davis, Dec. 30, 1864 (two letters), Rowland, *JDC*, 6:432–33; Crist, *PJD*, 11:320n.

12. Meeting between Davis and Blair, ibid., 11:315–25.

13. Abraham Lincoln to Blair, Jan. 18, 1865, in Roy P. Basler, ed., *The Collected Works of Abraham Lincoln*, 9 vols. (New Brunswick, N.J.: Rutgers University Press, 1953–55), 8:220–21.

14. Crist, *PJD*, 11:355–56, 379n. Charles W. Sanders, "Jefferson Davis and the Hampton Roads Peace Conference: 'To secure peace to the two countries,'" *Journal of Southern History* 63 (1997): 803–26, argues unconvincingly that Davis hoped the conference might succeed in achieving peace with independence.

15. Crist, *PJD*, 11:356.

16. Ulysses S. Grant to Edwin M. Stanton, Feb. 2, 1865, in Basler, *Collected Works of Lincoln*, 8:282.

17. Lincoln's instructions to Seward, Jan. 31, 1865, ibid., 8:279.

18. Rowland, *JDC*, 6:465–67.

19. Jones, *Rebel War Clerk's Diary*, 2:411, entry of Feb. 7, 1865; *Richmond Dispatch*, Feb. 7, 1865, quoted in John G. Nicolay and John Hay, *Abraham Lincoln: A History*, 10 vols. (New York: Century, 1890), 10:130–31.

20. *Richmond Examiner* and Stephens quoted in Cooper, *Davis*, 513.

21. *Richmond Dispatch* quoted in Ballard, *Long Shadow*, 20; Wiggins, *Journals of Gorgas*, 151, entry of Feb. 10, 1865; Jones, *Rebel War Clerk's Diary*, 2:411, entry of Feb. 6, 1865.

22. Thomas Robson Hay, "Lucius B. Northrop: Commissary General of the Confederacy," *Civil War History* 9 (1963): 19; Jeremy P. Felt, "Lucius B. Northrop and the Confederacy's Subsistence Department," *Virginia Magazine of History and Biography* 69 (1961), 190–92; Crist, *PJD*, 11:312n.

23. Howell Cobb to Davis, Jan. 20, 1865, Henry D. Clayton to Davis, Feb. 15, 1865, Crist, *PJD,* 11:343, 403.

24. Jones, *Rebel War Clerk's Diary,* 2:413, entry of Feb. 8, 1865; Rowland, *JDC,* 6:491–503.

25. Robert E. Lee to Davis, Feb. 23, 1865, Crist, *PJD,* 11:421 and 422n.

26. Jones, *Rebel War Clerk's Diary,* 2:343–44, entry of Dec. 1, 1864; Crist, *PJD,* 11:193–94. See also William C. Davis, *Jefferson Davis: The Man and His Hour* (New York: HarperCollins, 1991), 458; Woodworth, *Davis and Lee,* 254, 303.

27. E. B. Long, *The Civil War Day by Day: An Almanac, 1861–1865* (Garden City, N.Y.: Doubleday, 1971), 706.

28. Crist, *PJD,* 10:183n.

29. Benjamin F. Rollins to Davis, July 24, 1863, I. H. M. Barton to Davis, July 29, 1863, Leonidas N. Walthall to Davis, Aug. 11, 1863, ibid., 9:304, 312–13, 339–40.

30. *Montgomery Weekly Mail,* Sept. 2, 1863, *Mobile Register,* Nov. 26, 1863, in Robert F. Durden, *The Gray and the Black: The Confederate Debate on Emancipation* (Baton Rouge: Louisiana State University Press, 1972), 33, 44.

31. *O.R.,* ser. 1, vol. 52, pt. 2:586–92.

32. Ibid., pt. 2:598–99.

33. Maj. Gen. William H. T. Walker to Davis, Jan. 12, 1864, Isham G. Harris to Davis, Jan. 16, 1864, Crist, *PJD,* 10:170, 177–78.

34. Davis to Gen. Walker, Jan. 23, 1864, Rowland, *JDC,* 6:159–60; Crist, *PJD,* 10:178–79n.

35. Rowland, *JDC,* 6:394–97.

36. Crabtree and Patton, *"Journal of a Secesh Lady,"* 639, entry of Nov. 20, 1864.

37. *Richmond Examiner,* Nov. 8, 1864, *Charleston Mercury,* Nov. 12, 1864, in Durden, *The Gray and the Black,* 108–9, 112–13.

38. "Farmer" to Davis, Jan. 7, 1865, Samuel Clayton to Davis, Jan. 10, 1865, Crist, *PJD,* 11:285–86, 301.

39. Davis to John Forsyth, Feb. 21, 1865, ibid., 11:412–13.

40. David Yulee to Davis, Oct. 27, 1864, ibid., 11:125–26; Cobb to James Seddon, Jan. 8, 1865, forwarded to Davis with an endorsing cover letter from Seddon, Jan. 21, 1865, ibid., 11:347.

41. Mississippi congressman quoted in Durden, *The Gray and the Black,* 140; Louis T. Wigfall quoted in E. Merton Coulter, *The Confederate States of America, 1861–1865* (Baton Rouge: Louisiana State University Press, 1950), 268.

42. Lee to Andrew Hunter, Jan. 11, 1865, Lee to Ethelbert Barksdale, Feb. 18, 1865, in Durden, *The Gray and the Black,* 206–9.

43. Durden, *The Gray and the Black,* 268–70; George C. Rable, *The Confederate Republic: A Revolution Against Politics* (Chapel Hill: University of North Carolina Press, 1994), 295–96.

44. Davis to Lee, Mar. 13, 1865, Davis to William Smith, Mar. 30, 1865, Rowland, *JDC,* 6:513, 523; Davis to Lee, Apr. 1, 1865, Crist, *PJD,* 11:492.

45. Craig A. Bauer, "The Last Effort: The Secret Mission of the Confederate Diplomat, Duncan F. Kenner," *Louisiana History* 22 (1981): 71–75; Cooper, *Davis,* 514–15.

46. Frank Lawrence Owsley, *King Cotton Diplomacy: Foreign Relations of the Confederate States of America* (Chicago: University of Chicago Press, 1931), 550–61, quotation from p. 560.

47. Ballard, *Long Shadow,* 25.

48. Ibid., 22–23, 28; William C. Davis, *An Honorable Defeat: The Last*

Days of the Confederate Government (New York: Harcourt, 2001), 27–48.

49. Rowland, *JDC,* 6:386–87.

50. Crist, *PJD,* 11:430.

51. Davis to Braxton Bragg, Apr. 1, 1865, ibid., 11:489–90.

52. Rowland, *JDC,* 6:529–31.

53. Crist, *PJD,* 11:532.

54. John Dooley, quoted in Ballard, *Long Shadow,* 112.

ILLUSTRATION CREDITS

ILLUSTRATION CREDITS

INDEX

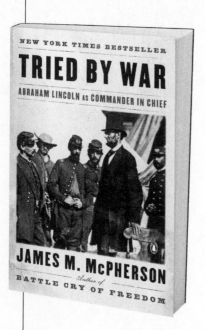